The Invisible Culture

The Invisible Culture
Communication in Classroom and Community on the Warm Springs Indian Reservation

Susan Urmston Philips
University of Arizona

WAVELAND
PRESS, INC.
Prospect Heights, Illinois

For information about this book, contact:
  Waveland Press, Inc.
  P.O. Box 400
  Prospect Heights, Illinois 60070
  (847) 634-0081
  www.waveland.com

Cover: Design on bag in twined weaving by the Wishram and Wasco Indians of Oregon and Washington, 19th century.

ISBN 0-88133-694-7

Printed in the United States of America

14   13   12   11   10

This book is dedicated to
my dear friend Velma Frank,
and to all her "kids."

Acknowledgments

Without the support and help of many people of the Warm Springs Confederated Tribes this study would not have been possible. In the fall of 1968, the late Vernon Jackson introduced me to other people in the tribal government who helped me, including Rudy Clements, Lloyd Smith, and Ken Smith. Vernon Jackson also made it possible for me to live on the reservation and arranged for my introduction to Madras School District administrators, who in turn opened the schools to me and introduced me to the concerned teachers who let me come into their classrooms. I was also supported by the friendship of Hiram Smith, Barbara Yaw and her family, Alice Florindo, Bessie and Phil Guerin and their family, and Velma Frank and her family.

My Ph.D. dissertation committee, Dell Hymes, Ward Good-enough, and Erving Goffman, gave useful criticisms of an earlier version of the book. Dell's own work on the Warm Springs Reservation opened the way for me in many ways.

Finally I was supported financially during the period of research by a graduate fellowship and a dissertation improvement grant from the National Science Foundation.

Contents

Introduction 1993

Theory and Practice

The Invisible Culture is a study of the organization of communication in face-to-face interaction among the Warm Springs Indians and of the consequences of that organization for the teaching and learning experiences of Warm Springs Indian children in and out of school. On the one hand, the book is intended to develop our understanding of the nature of human communication in face-to-face interaction, and of what is universal and culturally variable in human communication. On the other hand, this book is a critique of the ways in which Indian children are treated in American schools, where the organization of interaction places them in a subordinate position not only by virtue of their status as children and students relative to adult teachers, but also as Indians relative to the dominant Euro-American school culture imposed upon them through teachers' control of classroom interaction. Relatedly, the book has specific implications for the way in which teaching and learning in American classrooms can be changed to make school learning experiences less oppressive for ethnic minority children who learn how to learn in culturally diverse ways.

It is not accidental or coincidental that this ethnography has these two dimensions, for the book was deliberately fashioned to address both "theoretical" and "applied" concerns at the time it was written, in the 1970s. At that time, as I perceived it, "applied" work was not well-regarded within my discipline of anthropology. Many cultural and linguistic anthropologists viewed the applied work that was being done as theoretically weak and felt that researchers allowed their research agendas to be defined by others. Usually what was meant by "others" was the nation-state, or more specifically, its research funding agencies, whose agendas were viewed with suspicion from the political left. At that time I agreed that much applied work in anthropology was theoretically weak, but believed it was important for the social sciences to try to meet the promise they held out to our society to work on ideas with the potential to enhance our lives more than intellectually.

It seemed obvious to me that theory and practice should be connected and in a dynamic relationship in my chosen area of study, the ethnography of communication, and I endeavored to connect theory and practice in this book. I absolutely believe that work which aspires to change lives in our society for the better should be clearly and explicitly grounded in self-conscious theorizing about the nature of the activity which is the focus of change.

The question I address in this introduction is this: How does the book look ten years after its publication and twenty years after some of the ideas that shaped it took form? As the preceding paragraphs already suggest, the present intellectual context is one in which I find it easier to be explicit about the connections between theory and practice than I was at the time I wrote the book. When I look at the book now, I see a need to specify those connections, which is what much of this introduction is about.

Microethnography

The Invisible Culture has been interpreted by some people who have read it as representing a "micro" approach to educational issues within educational anthropology, presumably as opposed to a more "macro" approach. The book has been appreciated or castigated in ways intertwined with the researchers' conceptualizations of a micro approach and its value.

In my mind, the distinction between macro and micro analyses of social processes is associated with the emergence of social-interactional traditions in sociology under the influence of George Herbert Mead and Alfred Schutz and their descendants, Erving Goffman, Harold Garfinkel and Aaron Cicourel. In these traditions identity and meaning are constituted in human interaction. Microsociological research focuses on social processes in naturally occurring social interaction.

Within sociology such work has been criticized for its purported failure to both connect with and explain wider societal processes, or macro-sociological phenomena such as class, political institutions, and national economies. Some social interactionists have countered this criticism with efforts to conceptualize the macro-micro relationship productively. Interestingly, while the definition of *micro*sociological processes in such discussions is pretty stable and clear (they are face-to-face interactions), the definition of *macro*sociological processes is much less stable and clear.

From a micro point of view, the macrosociological can be conceptualized as an abstraction from or a theory about microsociological processes, as an accumulation of interactions, and as a relationship among such interactions. In other words, there is a real sense in which *only* micro-phenomena exist or happen, and macroanalyses are simply ways of conceptualizing relations among microphenomena.

In the 1960s, Joshua Fishman applied this sociological distinction to sociolinguistic work to differentiate macrosociolinguistic and micro-sociolinguistic research. He used the distinction roughly as the sociologists did, but limited the application of the distinction to work focusing on the language-society connection. In other words, microsociolinguistic research focused on language in human interaction, while macro-sociolinguistic work focused on language in broader societal organization.

In anthropology, and in education, studies of face-to-face interactional processes are sometimes characterized as microethnographic, and the term *microethnography* has been coined and used in these disciplines to distinguish it from traditional or classic ethnography. Traditional ethnography refers to the practice of living in a community for an extended period of time and engaging in participant observation in that community while a member of it. Through this process one comes to understand the activities one participates in from the point of view of the indigenous members of the community. In contrast, microethnographic research involves (1) the tape recording or videotaping of the naturally occurring activity in focused gatherings; (2) the representation of that activity in a transcription which minimally includes the speech of the participants in the activity, but may also include information about their nonverbal behavior; and (3) the close scrutiny of the transcripts with the goal of saying something about the nature of the human activity documented.

These methods have in common above all a commitment to the study of naturally occurring activity, as opposed to activity which would not have occurred without the intervention of the researcher in the form of interviews and experiments. There is a also a significant commitment in both methodologies to the researcher's direct experiencing of the phenomena she or he aspires to characterize.

The theoretical conceptualization of communication in face-to-face interaction in Chapter 1 of this book has very strong roots in microsociological and microsociolinguistic traditions. But methodologically, I see myself as using microethnography as part of a more traditional general ethnography that attempts to encompass the culture of a community, in this case conceptualized as a reservation, through self-conscious participant observation. To simply refer to this book as microethnography glosses over how little this study actually involved close analysis of transcripts, and how very much it relied on participant observation in the Warm Springs community and on plain noninteractive observation in the classroom. I stress this here because the analysis that makes up this book could not have come from classroom microethnography alone. To view this book as only a classroom microethnography would negate and ignore the contribution that the broader and more general ethnographic tradition can and does make to this study and to our understanding of human interaction and human socialization more generally.

Microethnography in Educational Anthropology

In recent years educational anthropologists have taken up the macro-micro distinction and created a polarization between work using macrosociological theory and ethnographic methods and work using microsociological theories of social interaction and microethnographic methods. In general, those claiming to adhere to some kind of macro position, however vaguely defined, have attacked microethnographers as offering only an incomplete and nonuniversal account or explanation of ethnic minority failure in schools. Microethnographers have countered with arguments for the value of the studies they do. While this debate has stimulated discussion within educational anthropology, I feel both sides have really allowed mischaracterizations of microethnography that retard the theoretical and practical development of this anthropological subdisciplinary interest to flourish.

First, microethnography is rarely defined or characterized in these critiques. Microethnographic method tends to be implicitly equated with the close analysis of a single activity, for example one classroom lesson. The enormous diversity in the ways in which recordings and transcriptions of activities have been used by anthropologists doing microethnographic work is simply ignored or glossed over.

Critics identified with more macroanalytic traditions claim that they discovered or invented the comparative method in educational research that addresses the problems of ethnic minority children. It is quite common, however, for multiple activities which are taped repeatedly to constitute the data base of microethnographers focusing on the educational experience of ethnic minorities. It has also been characteristic of this work since its inception in the late 1960s to systematically employ the comparative method in the anthropological tradition that identifies natural experiments existing in naturally occurring behavior. Attention has focused on the comparison of ethnic groups and on different activities of those groups in the recording of multiple activities. Thus, Fred Erickson systematically videotaped different ethnic combinations of junior college counselors and students for his and Jeffry Schultz's book *The Counselor as Gatekeeper*. Similarly, in this study of Warm Springs, I systematically compared classrooms of Indian children with classrooms of Anglo children in a carefully selected sampling of different grade levels and participant structures. If anything, then, macroanalytic educational ethnographers have acquired the comparative method from microethnographers, rather than the other way around.

Macroanalysts have also created the impression that researchers are either ethnographers or microethnographers only. In reality, traditional ethnography and microethnography are commonly carried out together. As I have already noted, this is true of my own study on the Warm Springs Reservation. It is also true of Shirley Heath's research forming the basis for *Ways with Words*. The use of microethnographic methods in the context of traditional ethnography is also characteristic of almost all of the language socialization research growing out of the ethnography of communication interest in communicative competence, most notably in the work of Karen Watson-Gegeo, Elinor Ochs and Bambi Schieffelin.

Those who use microethnography in the context of the traditional ethnographic experience have often done so because of the problems they perceive with so-called holism, notably its lack of accountability to any identifiable or retrievable body of data. In reality, in ethnographic work, there has existed for some time a plethora of very specific methods associated with specific subdisciplinary interests that facilitate an accountability not possible through participant observation and field notes, regardless of the undeniable value of those traditional methods. This point is also ignored and obscured by the macro-micro polarization.

It has also been suggested that microethnographic work is, in its cultural and social structuralism, overly deterministic, ignoring the locally negotiated historical situatedness of the phenomena it documents. And it has also been said that microethnographers have only recognized the potential for transformation of the circumstances they document — the potential for ethnic minorities to be freed from the grip of oppression in schools — by having it pointed out to them by macroanalysts. It is true that some microethnographic work is very structural, very taken with the discovery of different "systems" for organizing interaction. Certainly my own work conceptualizes Warm Springs Indians and Anglos as having different systems for regulating talk. And for me personally this stretch for the normative, for the pattern, is almost irresistible. It is also equally true that structuralism is far from absent in the work of its critics. Pattern and regularity should not be seen as antithetical to, or precluding conceptualization of, individual agency and the local constructions of social realities.

There is also much more about the local negotiation of meaning in microethnographic work than is recognized in the criticisms of its structuralism. Most importantly, this work shows how relations of authority and power are locally contructed in face-to-face interaction. Those with control over the regulation of talk have more influence over the social reality constructed by cointeractants than those who lack such control.

The organization of interaction in classrooms allocates control over interactions to teachers, which in turn enables them to define the reality of the situation, its meaning, what "really" happened. The same control and power to define reality is given to bureaucrats who wield it over their clients across a wide range of institutional settings such as courts and clinics. This bureaucrat-client relationship of dominant to subordinate both mirrors and encompasses many other relationships of domination and subordination in this country, obviously here, that of Anglo to ethnic minority person, but also of man to woman, colonizer to colonized, and middle class to working class.

In other words, the microethnographic tradition in anthropology and sociology that began with classroom research has shown broadly, clearly and coherently the ways in which dominant-subordinate relationships are formed in face-to-face interaction. This work situates the exercise of power in practice, rather than abstracting it from practice as structural theories do.

And contrary to the macroanalytical claims that the work in this tradition has little or nothing to say about power, racism, or locally situated realities, microethnographic work, including *The Invisible Culture*, conceptualizes the experience of the ethnic minority child in school as embedded in power relationships. Thus, microethnographic studies do not just argue, as has sometimes been claimed, that "culture differences" explain why ethnic minority children have difficulties in school. Rather, they show how ethnic minority children are constituted, indeed are created, as having difficulties, through and by virtue of classroom organization of interaction. They make the point that this is not some objective reality, not a fact, but rather a consequence of the way in which ethnic minority children are incorporated into classroom interactions. "Failure" does not come about because these children are members of an involuntary ethnic minority and have developed a psychological orientation toward school through which they prevent themselves from succeeding. This is something that is *done to* children by teachers who define them in this way.

This theory of power relationships is one very closely connected to the popular political culture of the 1960s that gave birth to it. The influence of the women's movement, in which it was argued that men exercise power over women partly through their control of face-to-face interactions, is particularly evident in the widely shared characterization of power relationships in microethnographic work. An important aspect of this characterization of power relationships is that it takes the blame off of the victims of racism and places it on the Euro-Americans or Anglos who are in positions of domination in schools and other bureaucracies that encompass ethnic minorities. This view has direct implications for change in the classroom and the other institutional settings it focuses on. It argues for the modification of the organization of interaction in these contexts in ways that lessen the controlling and defining roles of the teacher (or doctor or lawyer) and give more agency to the students (or patients or witnesses).

This book makes that argument when it shows how much more engaged and productive Warm Springs Indian children are when they are learning in participant structures over which they have more control. The same kind of argument has been made for the part-Hawaiian children whose learning was positively influenced in the Kamehameha Learning Project when they were allowed to tell stories in school cooperatively as Karen Watson-Gegeo had found them doing in the community. Fred Erickson has referred to such actions as changes of ''least difference,'' arguing that small changes can make an enormous difference in the learning experience of the child.

Thus, the earlier-mentioned macroanalytic position that structuralism in microethnographic work has made it overdeterministic and unable to allow for change until the possibility for change was pointed out by historically situated macroanalysis is simply wrong. If anything, microethnographers, with our phenomenological bent, have made the institutionalized racism at issue here seem more potentially easily done away with than it has in fact been. But at least microethnographers have developed models of teaching and learning from which specific implications for practice can be derived; they have related theory to practice. Macrosociological accounts of ethnic school ''failure,'' in all their ephemerality, cannot do this.

The microethnographic work that focuses on the ways in which children are controlled and defined by teachers, particularly ethnic minority children, has also been criticized for characterizing children as if they had no agency whatsoever, as if the need to change interactions to give students more agency ignored what agency they have. This criticism has come from Vygotskians, who see an inherent agency in the child as a learner much as Chomsky does. It has also come from Marx-influenced work that argues it is demeaning to American ethnic minorities and other colonized populations to write about them as if they were totally passive victims with no capacity to resist or contribute to their own destiny.

I agree with this criticism. A view that gives agency to children is also more consistent with a conception of meaning in face-to-face inter-action as jointly negotiated. On the other hand, too much attention to the inherent agency of the child as learner and to the resistance of ethnic minorities to domination by the white majority can also obscure how very little agency and resistance is actually possible for people in subordinated positions before they are cast out of the activity in which they are exercising their agency, as with Paul Willis' lads in *Learning to Labour*.

At this point I would like to return to the idea raised at the beginning of this section that microethnographic research cannot explain ethnic minority school failure. Here I must say that I do not think it was ever meant to provide a complete account of what happens to ethnic minority children in school, but rather to contribute a necessary component of such an account that had been missing. Because humans learn how to be humans in face-to-face interaction, it is necessary to include micro-ethnographic method and theory in any account of this process. And as I have mentioned above, the microethnographic tradition also has some advantages or strengths lacking in macroanalytic traditions: it offers accountability to a data base. That is, it claims to characterize a body of data from tapes and transcripts to which others can have access so as to verify the analysis, and it has demonstrated the ability to link theory to practice so that explicit recommendations for social change can follow from the conceptualization of the phenomena studied.

It is relevant to ask here whether the goal that is demanded of micro-ethnographic research, i.e., that it account for ethnic minority school failure, should indeed be the main goal of educational anthropology. I personally feel this is far too narrow a focus. My vision of educational anthropology is that it should contextualize formal schooling as one kind of socialization within a perspective in which socialization in and out of schools, for all human beings, in all nations, is appropriate subject matter.

It is also relevant to ask whether the whole microethnographic tradition, which encompasses most of linguistic anthropology today, as well as much educational anthropology, and is increasingly attracting other kinds of cultural anthropologists, can appropriately be judged on the basis of whether it explains ethnic minority school failure. I think not. In the present intellectual climate in the humanities and social sciences, in which human social *practice*, rather than human society or the individual human mind, has been identified as the locus of human culture, only microethnography, in its combined theoretical and methodological dimensions, examines practice closely. Thus, microethnography has great promise for shedding light on the nature of culture in practice. Also at present, microethnography threatens to obviate its own definition and to eliminate or completely reconceptualize the macro-micro relationship by building a macroanalytic theory through analysis of the ways in which different specific interactions are related to each other. This is done, for example, in the book *Handicapping the Handicapped* by Hugh (Bud) Mehan, Alma Hetweck and J. Lee Meihls.

I am very pleased that Waveland Press has provided the opportunity for this reprinting of *The Invisible Culture* as an example of a traditional ethnography in which microethnographic method and theory figure prominently. And I am grateful to the friends and colleagues who encouraged me to seek its reprinting, particularly to Steve Grubis, Elinor Ochs, Ray Barnhardt, Bambi Schieffelin, Pamela Bunte and Roberto Carrasco.

Part I
Introduction

1

Verbal and Nonverbal Communication in the Socialization of Children

An Anthropological Approach to Language Socialization

Since the 1950s there has been a tangible commitment on the part of the United States federal government to increase ethnic minority children's access to the knowledge schools offer, as a means toward equalizing educational opportunities, but we still have far to go. There is a need for a model of child socialization that works for all children, coupled with a financial commitment to the educational implementation of that model.

One model of socialization that is appealing in part because of its potential relevance for all children is Dell Hymes' concept of communicative competence (Hymes, 1967). The concept was developed in part in response or reaction to Noam Chomsky's concept of linguistic competence as knowledge of grammar. Hymes argued that the native speaker's intuitions about grammatical acceptibility cannot be separated from sociocultural knowledge about the situational or contextual appropriateness of an utterance. Communicative competence, then, refers to the ability of a member of a given culture to use language in a socially appropriate manner (Goodenough, 1976) in the service of social ends and social meanings.

From an anthropological point of view, this perspective is part of a theory of socialization. In cultural terms, socialization is the enculturation or transmission of cultural knowledge. The transmission of cultural knowledge is accomplished through language use (White, 1949), or more broadly, through situated face-to-face interaction (Goffman, 1963; Goodenough, 1976). Thus understanding of the nature of communicative competence should give us insight into factors affecting the transmission of culture.

Just as there is a developmental sequence in the acquisition of linguistic competence that has both universal and variable properties, so too there is a developmental sequence in the acquisition of communicative competence that has both universal and variable dimensions. One problem with our educational system is that a shared developmental sequence in the preschool enculturation of children is assumed, when in fact that developmental sequence may be culturally diverse in ways as yet unacknowledged by curriculum developers.

In this book, I argue that the children of the Warm Springs Indian Reservation are enculturated in their preschool years into modes of organizing the transmission of verbal messages that are culturally different from those of Anglo middle-class children. I argue that *this difference makes it more difficult for them to then comprehend verbal messages conveyed through the American school's Anglo middle-class modes of organizing classroom interaction.*

These patterns in the organization of communication involve both verbal and nonverbal behavior. The book focuses on cultural variation in the integration of information in the visual and auditory channels, both in general, and more specifically, in the structuring of attention and the regulation of turns at talk.

The Relation Between Verbal and Nonverbal Behavior in Human Communication

When we consider the significance and attention given to language by anthropologists, comparatively little attention or significance has been attached to nonverbal behavior, or to its contributions to the communication of cultural information. Our nonverbal and paralinguistic behaviors have rightly been viewed as those aspects of our communicative system which have more in common with the communication systems of other primates, while language has been treated as that which is distinctive to humans. At the same time, one significant point that has been made about nonverbal behavior by anthropologists is that a great deal of it is culturally patterned, or learned, like language (Birdwhistell, 1970; Hall, 1966; Efron, 1941,

LaBarre, 1947). Even so, the contributions of nonverbal behavior to our communicative process have been relatively neglected.

In attempting to characterize the main functions of nonverbal behavior in human communication, it is useful to distinguish between interaction that is organized primarily through human physical activity, and interaction that is organized through talk. In interaction that is shaped and derives its meaning largely from physical activity, as in the joint physical labor of such diverse activities as preparing a field for cultivation, moving a couch, and engaging in a ritual dance, nonverbal behavior is the primary source of information, and provides the context for any talk which occurs. In interaction that is structured through talk, where talk itself is the context for other talk, gross movement is reduced to that involved in people moving in and out of the range of talk. At the same time, whenever people are within close enough range to talk to one another directly, they are also within seeing range of one another, given the absence of physical and light barriers. In discussing the functions of nonverbal communication here, I will be primarily concerned with its functions in interaction structured through talk.

Nonverbal behavior has three basic functions in interaction regulated through talk. First, it conveys information about the emotional states of participants in talk through body positioning, facial expression, and gestural pattern. Ekman (1974) and Chevalier-Skolnikoff (1974) have taken the position that the behaviors associated with emotional states such as anger and joy are universal to the human species, and may be shared with our primate relatives.

A second function of nonverbal behavior is the provision of basic social information about one's cointeractants and oneself, through the manipulation of dress and appearance. Gender and ethnicity are both examples of kinds of basic social information that are conveyed through nonverbal behavior in a way that allows parties to talk to take that information into consideration in deciding how to address one another (Philips, 1980).

The third basic function of nonverbal behavior, and the one with which this book is concerned, is the facilitation of the regulation of talk (Duncan, 1972; Kendon, 1967). For a linguistic message to be sent successfully, it is crucial that the speaker secure the attention of the hearer. In other words, it is necessary that the hearer recognize that he is the addressed recipient of the linguistic message. The speaker must also be made aware that the hearer recognizes him as the addressor.

More specifically, the following conditions must be met for the successful sending of a message: (1) The speaker must behave in such a way as to attract the attention of the hearer. He must also convey to the hearer that the hearer is the person being addressed. The speaker must, then, designate an addressed recipient. (2) The hearer must identify the speaker and recognize that the speaker is designating him as the addressed recipient. (3) Once the hearer has identified the speaker he must behave in such a way as to convey that he is attending, and, more specifically, that he is attending to the speaker. He must then designate his addressor. (4) Finally, the speaker must determine that he has been designated as the addressor, or that he has the attention of his designated listener. In so doing, the speaker may also be said to be sometimes identifying his listener. This is particularly true when there are several hearers, or potential addressed recipients present, and the speaker is searching to find one or some who are paying attention to him, so that he may justify continuing to speak.

It should be apparent that there are both productive and receptive dimensions to the conditions that speaker and hearer must meet in order for a message to be successfully sent. Productively, the speaker must behave so as to designate a hearer as his addressed recipient, and the hearer must behave so as to designate a speaker as his addressor. Receptively, the hearer must recognize that he is being addressed, and the speaker must recognize that he is being attended to.

The set of patterned actions by speaker and hearer that occur in order that the conditions for successful transmission of linguistic messages may be met will be referred to as the *attention structure* of human interaction. The concept and the term are borrowed from the work of M.R.A. Chance (Chance, 1962; Chance and Larsen, 1975), who used it to explain spatial positioning in primate dominance hierarchies. Chance argued that less dominant members of the group position themselves so that they can visually monitor the more dominant animals. Shafton (1976:48) has criticized Chance for his failure to characterize the behavior of the less dominant animals as well. Shafton maintains that the less dominant animals gaze at the more dominant to monitor their behavior, but look away to avoid the connotation of threat when the more dominant gaze in their direction. By contrast the more dominant animals have no need to monitor the behavior of the less dominant, but they are free to gaze at will because threat of the gaze will not be challenged by the less dominant members of the group.

As both Shafton and Pitcairn and Eibl-Eibesfeldt (1976:97) have pointed out, one of the things that distinguishes human nonverbal behavior from that of other primates is the extent to which humans gaze freely into one another's faces. Pitcairn and Eibl-Eibesfeldt attribute this difference to the evolution of language and speech, pointing out the important role gaze plays in the regulation of talk, as evidenced by Kendon's (1967) work. The human attention structure, then, is behaviorally quite different from that of other primates,* but still concerned with the behavioral means used by humans to determine who is paying attention to whom. Yet in spite of the differences betweem humans and other primates, the use of the concept attention structure is intended to convey the notion of continuity within the primate order between humans and other primates in the organization of communication in face-to-face interaction.

While the conditions that must be met to successfully transmit a linguistic message in human interaction are universal, the behavioral means for meeting those conditions are not. *Attention may be captured and conveyed in either or both the auditory and the visual channel and the behavioral means for accomplishing these ends may vary.* My purpose here is to provide a comparative framework detailing the sources of cultural variability in the behavioral production of the attention structure of human interaction. Once the potential sources of variability have been detailed, it will be easier to understand why the attention structure of Warm Springs Indians' interaction differs in the ways that it does from the attention structure of persons from a white middle-class background.

The Behavioral Means for Securing and Conveying Attention

Designation of Addressed Recipient

Let us consider first the ways in which a speaker can attract the attention of a hearer and designate him as an addressee in the auditory and visual channels.

In the *auditory* channel, talk itself is a bid for attention. Because it is under the voluntary control of the speaker, talk is always intentional, and its production almost always indicates that the speaker is either seeking an audience or assumes he has one. The speaker has a number of linguistic means for identifying or designating those

---

* Some of the ethological research that reflects the influence of Chance's concept of attention structures (e.g., Chance and Larson, 1976) suggests that human interaction *is* like that of other primates, in being hierarchically organized. But this finding may be due to the selective focus of the researchers, and/or may be subject to situational and cultural variation.

whom he seeks as addressed recipients. The speaker may, of course, name the recipient (or recipients). But more commonly the speaker is likely to designate an addressed recipient through the form of the utterance. This is often accomplished when an utterance is meaningful to only some of those present because only they have the shared background knowledge from outside the immediate context to be able to make sense of what is said. There are other verbal means of designating an addressed recipient. Blount (1972), for example, suggests that the higher pitch range of baby talk designates a baby as the addressed recipient.

In the *visual* channel, the speaker may attract the attention of a hearer through speaker-specific body movements. The movements most specific to speakers and most conspicuous are the hand gestures that accompany talk, but lip movement, head bobbing, and pivoting of the trunk of the body may also attract the attention of others.

The designation of an addressed recipient in the visual channel is most often accomplished by gaze direction: the speaker looks into the face of the person or persons the utterance is directed to. Body alignment may also serve to designate the addressed recipient in that a speaker is likely to most directly face those being addressed. As we will see in the later description of Warm Springs communicative behavior, the nature of verbal and visual designation of addressed recipient varies cross-culturally in a variety of ways. As a consequence of this a person from one culture may sometimes not recognize when a person from another culture is designating him as the person to whom a linguistic message is being sent.

Hearer Recognition of Addressor

For the successful transmission of a verbal message, the hearer must recognize being selected as an addressed recipient, or else will not attend to what the speaker is saying. In part this entails the recognition that the designating activities of the speaker are meant for the hearer. One crucial aspect of that recognition that requires more attention here is the identification of the speaker. There are several reasons why the hearer may need to identify the speaker. First, if the hearer's attention has been attracted and designation is conveyed by the speaker in the auditory channel, the hearer may need to locate and identify the speaker visually, in order to confirm that verbal designation, by determining whether the speaker is gazing at him. Second, as discussed earlier, the hearer needs to know the individual identity of the speaker in order to assign meaning to the utterance. Finally, and most importantly for the purposes of the attention structure, the hearer needs to identify the addressor in order to convey to the right person that attention is being paid to the verbal message.

In the auditory channel, speaker identification may be accomplished through recognition of the individual's voice quality, although this will be difficult if there are many people present, or if the person is not well known. The structure of the utterance may also reveal the individual identity of the speaker, but the reliability of this source of information also depends on how long the speaker has been known, and how long the present interaction has been ongoing.

Visual identification is easier than auditory identification because of the finer discriminatory powers of the eyes. Visual identification would entail attention to the same speaker body movements that were described as attracting attention—hand gestures, head movements, and alignment shifts. The hearer's recognition of the speaker then depends on the receptive competence to decode the speaker's behavior, or productive competence in conveying who is being addressed. And as with productive competence, the nature of the receptive competence is culturally variable. Thus hearers vary across cultures regarding the behaviors on which they selectively focus their eyes and ears, and in the interpretations made of what they see and hear.

Designation of Addressor

The hearer must behave in a way that conveys attention, and at the same time behave so as to designate who attention is being paid to, if the speaker is to know that his or her words are being received.

Attention can be conveyed in the auditory channel in several ways. It can be conveyed negatively through silence on the part of the hearer. Silence could at least convey that the person being addressed is capable of receiving the message, while a person who was speaking would be less capable of reception. Attention can also be conveyed in the auditory channel through "back channel work" (Yngve, 1970), such as the occasional "mmm humms" and "yeses" produced by white middle-class Americans in response to what the speaker is saying. Finally, attention can be conveyed in the auditory channel through the hearer's response to what the speaker has said. Here the response may indicate, through its appropriateness and the ways in which it is tied to and structurally dependent on the preceding utterance, that the hearer has heard what the speaker said (Sacks, 1967).

In the visual channel, the hearer may designate attention to the speaker by gaze at the speaker, and by body movement patterns that are associated with listening. For example, Condon and Ogston (1971) maintain that the hearer's smallest body movements are in rhythm with the speaker's speech. And head nodding to convey attention is a specific gesture in American culture associated with conveying attention to a speaker. Once again, however, as we will see in describing Warm Springs behavior, listening behavior varies cross-culturally.

Speaker Recognition of Addressed Recipient

The final condition that must be met for a linguistic message to be transmitted successfully is that the speaker realize that he has been attended to. In general, this requires that the speaker focus on the various ways in which the hearer is paying attention—that the speaker be able to decode the message from the hearer conveyed in the ways just discussed. It is necessary here only to note further that the speaker's recognition that he has someone's attention is often the first step rather than the last step in the successful transmission of a message. In other words, the speaker often identifies and recognizes an addressed receiver—someone who is paying attention—*before* the speaker begins to speak. Here too, the nature of the speaker's receptive competence in recognizing who is conveying attention will vary cross-culturally in the selective attention paid to hearers' behavior.

From the preceding discussion, it should be apparent that either or both channels may be used in signaling attention of the speaker to the hearer and the hearer to the speaker. In the main body of this book, attention will focus on the ways in which the choices between the visual and auditory channels made by the Warm Springs Indians differ from those made by Anglos. The people of Warm Springs use the visual channel more than Anglos do; they use different behavioral means for conveying attention within the channel chosen; and where they use the *same* behavioral means, those means are used in different frequencies.

Among both Indians and Anglos, individuals differ in the frequency with which they use one channel rather than the other, and in the frequency with which they use particular signals within a given channel. This variation conveys information about social role and personality. The comparison between Anglo and Indian children's behavior in the Anglo classroom will consider this sort of variation.

But before turning to the treatment of cultural variation in attention structuring, it will be useful to provide an account of the plan of the book.

The Plan of the Book

The book is divided into three parts. Part I is comprised of this first chapter, which develops the framework within which Warm Springs Indian children's classroom experiences will be discussed, and Chapter 2, which describes the rationale for and nature of the data-gathering processes that yielded the information on which the analysis is based.

Part II focuses on the Warm Springs community environment that provides the Indian children with six years of preschool socialization with which they enter school. It describes what the children learn about the relative functions of the visual and auditory channels of communication, and the appropriate manner in which to use both channels in conveying attention and getting the floor to speak.

Part III focuses on the Indian children in the grammar school environment. It compares both their academic performance and their communicative behavior with that of Anglo children in a nearby off-reservation school, and draws on Part II to explain the differences in communicative behavior of the two cultural groupings of children.

Part II discusses the Indian children's early socialization for communication from three different points of view. Chapter 3 describes some basic features of the social organization of the Warm Springs Indian Reservation in central Oregon. The main purpose and focus of that description is to show how it is possible for children who speak English and who live in a material environment that is overwhelmingly Western in form can still grow up in a world where by far the majority of their enculturation experience comes from interaction with other Indians. Thus the school is still the main source of contact with mainstream Anglo culture.

Chapter 4 describes some important features of the communicative behavior of the Warm Springs adults who are the primary socializers and role models for the Warm Springs children during their preschool years.

Chapter 5 focuses on the behavior that Warm Springs adults and older children direct toward babies and young children, which encourages them to develop the same patterns of communicative behavior that the adults themselves display.

Thus Part II provides first a discussion of the reason why Indian children's role models come from so segregated an Indian network. Then an account of the communicative behavior of those role models is provided. And finally there is an account of the more focused socializing efforts by members of the Indian community that cause the Warm Springs children to become like their peers and elders.

Part III, Chapter 6, also begins with a discussion of social organization but focuses on the *interactional* organization of classroom activity. The purpose of this description is to provide a framework within which Indian and Anglo first and sixth graders' communicative behavior can be compared.

Chapter 7 describes some of the major sources of evidence that Indian children's academic comprehension is impaired by the transmission of knowledge through modes of communicative behavior that are culturally alien and uncommon in their experience.

Finally, in Chapter 8 the implications of this study for education practice are drawn.

The book is called *The Invisible Culture* because communicative patterns lack the tangible visible quality of houses, clothing, and tools, so that it is less easy to recognize their existence as culturally distinct phenomena. The purpose of the book is to render that invisible culture visible through description of its nature in the Warm Springs community and reconstruction of its impact in the classroom.

2

Research Methodology

The purpose of this chapter is to discuss briefly the ways in which the research design and methods for gathering data on which this book is based represent an anthropological approach to interaction. The discussion to follow will consider the purpose of the study, the use of participant observation as the key method for gathering data, and the particular features of the research design that made it possible to carry out the kind of analysis that characterizes the book.

The Purpose of the Study

The research on which this book is based was developed and carried out during the period from the fall of 1968, when contact was first established with the Warm Springs tribal administration, through the spring of 1973, with the bulk of the data gathered from the fall of 1969 to the spring of 1971, when I lived on the reservation. Because the research plan was developed during a period when I was regularly visiting the reservation, it was possible to take advantage of actual knowledge of the field situation and of the concerns of the tribal administration in developing the research.

The general purpose of the research was to explore in an openended fashion the ways in which Warm Springs Indians' use of language was culturally distinctive. The fact that most of the tribal members spoke English as their first language was advantageous for the research. It allowed for the study of cultural differences in language use that could be separated from the structure of the language itself. And Dell Hymes' accounts (1966, 1968) of the regional Indians' mythology, distinctive styles of storytelling, made it clear that there were ways in which Warm Springs people's use of English differed from that of Anglos.

There was also some research that the tribe had paid to have done (Zentner, 1960) indicating that while the Indian children tended to do more poorly than their Anglo counterparts on achievement tests in all skill areas, their poorest scores were in language-related skill areas. Thus it seemed worthwhile to explore the possibility that cultural differences in language use were contributing to the difficulties the Indian children were having in school. I approached the tribal administration with the concern to make my sociolinguistic research useful to them, and my proposal to focus on educational problems was greeted with enthusiasm by the tribal manager.

It was with these general concerns in mind that the research proposal was developed.

Participant Observation

A number of data-gathering techniques were used to obtain the information on which the analysis presented herein is based. However, the method that characterizes the study is *participant observation*. This term means several things to anthropologists. It can refer roughly to the experience of living with the group of people one is studying, as we are taught Malinowski did; it can refer to the investigator's occupying a position in the social structure as a way of learning about it, which is the classic sense in which the phrase is used; and it is sometimes used to refer more generally to the direct untampering observation of human interaction.

In all three senses of the term, participant observation is very closely associated with the distinctive anthropological activity of "doing ethnography." And even though researchers from other disciplines sometimes use participant observation as a research technique, anthropologists rely more heavily on it than other social scientists. Participant observation is also closely associated with research done in the manner of British anthropologists of the period when the influence of Radcliffe-Brown and structural functionalism was greatest in this country. In this context, participant observation is sometimes presented as a field research technique that is superior to the informant interviewing done by American anthropologists studying North American Indian culture in the 1920s and 1930s, and to the sending out of questionnaires that characterized the armchair anthropology of the 19th century.

In fact, of course, we continue to use a diversity of field research methods, each of which is particularly well suited for getting a certain type of information. What is relevant here is that of the traditional means for gathering data, participant observation is best suited for studying face-to-face interaction. Mailed questionnaires do not entail any direct contact with the people being studied. Interviewing becomes less and less like the interaction in which people regularly engage as it is more structured. Both tape recording and videotaping, however, can be seen as mechanical extensions of the observation process that promise to revolutionize the study of interaction.

Although the research on which this study is based was carried out through participant observation, there was considerable variation in the way in which the observation was carried out. In school classrooms I sat off to the side and observed and took notes during the first period of several months of data collection. I followed the children wherever they went during their school day, including the cafeteria at lunch and the playground during recess. I purposefully did not actively seek direct involvement with the children. I did not want to alter the quality of the interaction through my own participation. I also wanted to be free to focus my attention as I chose, and not to have my observational capacities limited by the need to participate. The bulk of my classroom data come from this process, but I also repeatedly informally interviewed the teachers in the classes where I observed, questioning them about what I had been observing. In my second period of observation in the schools, I tape recorded a number of encounters, and took notes as I taped.

In the Warm Springs community my activities consisted of visiting with people in their homes, traveling around the reservation with them, and attending community events open to the public, mixing varying degrees of participation with observation, and informally questioning the people I spent time with about whatever was necessary to make sense of reservation life.

At one time I attempted to develop a set of questions to interview the parents of the Indian children I was observing in school about the ways in which they trained and disciplined their children. For reasons that should be clear from later chapters, this interviewing was not successful and I abandoned the effort.

Classroom Research: Four Classrooms

As may be apparent from the preceding discussion, at the core of the data collection were periods of alternation between observation in the community and observation in the schools. The selection of classrooms to observe was designed to make it possible to determine what aspects of behavior were actually due to the Indian cultural background of the Warm Springs Indian children, rather than to some other aspect of their social environment.

An Explicit Comparison of Anglo and Indian Classes

Two of the classrooms in which observation was carried out were in the Warm Springs grade school, where 95 percent of the students were Indian children who lived on the reservation. The other two classrooms were in grade schools in the nearby off-reservation town of Madras, where at least 95 percent of the students were Anglo.

Throughout the book the non-Indian children, and the cultural background they bring with them to school, are referred to as Anglo. The term is not ideally appropriate because it denotes things English or British and the non-Indian children of central Oregon are clearly not English. But white denotes color and when used to refer to people is a racial term, whereas this study is dealing with culturally based differences. Anglo, by contrast, is a cultural term and is used in the United States to refer to people descended from English ancestors whose culture shows the strong influence of that English heritage.

There were several reasons for carrying out an explicit comparison of Anglo and Indian children's classroom behavior. First, and most importantly, such a comparison is necessary where the hypothesis is that the Indian students' difficulties in school are related to their cultural background. Cultural background cannot be a key causal factor unless the Indian children are in fact culturally different from the Anglo children who do not have difficulties. It was necessary first to establish whether such cultural differences could be identified in the children's behavior before considering whether the differences were related to the learning problems of the Indian students in any way.

Some readers may be willing to *assume* such cultural differences. However, it is not clear how much Indian culture remains after generation of efforts on the part of Anglos to eradicate that culture and assimilate the Indians into the mainstream culture. Cultural distinctiveness of the Indian children was little recognized by the teachers and administrators in the school district that encompassed the Warm Springs reservation. And while the tribal education department urged the school personnel to learn more about Indian culture as a key to understanding the children and improving their skills in school subjects, many older Indians declared there was little left of the old ways: Western European–derived clothing, housing, and occupations were the norm, and English was the dominant language. It was particularly unclear what cultural differences might exist in the area of language use, because language use as an aspect of cultural behavior had been so little studied in a systematic fashion.

A second reason for explicit Anglo-Indian comparison was the possibility that the Indian students might behave in a manner unfamiliar to the investigator due to the influence on the Indian children of the unfamiliar local or regional Anglo culture. Thus it was important to compare the Warm Springs children with children from the nearby town of Madras, rather than, say, children from urban Portland, Oregon, to distinguish that local Anglo influence from Indian culture.

A third reason for the comparison of Anglo and Indian students was my belief that such a comparison would be implicit in the research even if the Anglo students were not observed, and the comparison was more likely to be accurate if it was made explicit. Although difficult to prove, it seems likely that whenever ethnographic description focuses on some aspect of behavior that has been little studied, as was the case here with the focus on language use, it is apt to deal primarily with how the people in question differ from ourselves. Such behavior is more noticeable than behavior that we are already familiar with, and it more certainly qualifies as learned— i.e., as "cultural"—behavior. Only after some such descriptions have been made is a truly cross-cultural comparison possible.

One consequence of this comparison of Anglo and Indian children is an emphasis on how they differ and a neglect of how they are similar. Some Indian adults expressed discomfort with the emphasis on cultural differences between Anglos and Indians stressed by other Warm Springs adults. The experience of most tribal members was that all of the ways in which they were perceived as different by Anglos were stigmatized, so that "different" had negative connotations. There was also a very humanistic view held by some Warm Springs adults that only by stressing the similarities between Anglos and Indians would it be possible to get along with them, and improve relationships between the two groups. It is also true that even the ways in which Indians are like Anglos are still part of being "Indian." Nevertheless, if Indian and Anglo students

perform differently at classroom tasks, it is only through examina-
tion of the nature of the differences, not the similarities, in their behavior that the differences in classroom performance can be understood.

A Comparison of First and Sixth Graders

In both the Warm Springs grade school on the reservation and the
Madras grade schools off the reservation, observations were carried
out in both first- and sixth-grade classrooms. There were several
reasons for including classrooms at those two quite different levels.
First, and most importantly, one purpose of the comparison of students at two different grade levels was to isolate or separate the developmental process of acquiring communicative competence from
the phenomenon of more general cultural difference. Had the
observations been carried out for only one age group, differences between the Anglo and Indian groups could have been quite age-
specific rather than enduring. At the same time, it was hoped that
the age difference, in conjunction with community data, might provide some preliminary information on developmental sequences in
the acquisition of interactional competence.

Second, it seemed likely that the children of different ages
would have been influenced in varying degrees by the school environment itself. The first graders were the ones likely to have been
least influenced by the classroom's Anglo-derived organization of interaction, while the sixth graders were likely to have been the most
influenced by contact with the school. By looking at both ages, it
was hoped that the effect of school on the children's behavior could
be determined.

Finally, there were some notions about patterns in Indian education that could be tested by carrying out a comparison of the two
different age groups. First, both an older literature on Indian education (see Berry, 1968) and the teachers at the Warm Springs grade
school suggested that there was a sudden dramatic decline in Indian
children's school performance after three years in school. The literature indicated that Indian children performed above national norms
on achievement tests until the fourth grade, when there was a sharp
drop in the scores, which continued to get lower and lower through
the remaining grades. In the Warm Springs grade school there was
thought to be a language-use counterpart to this pattern; many
teachers at the school said that the Indian children were quite talka-
tive until the fourth grade, when they suddenly became very silent
and withdrawn, much to the teachers' dismay. I wanted to see if I

could observe this phenomenon, and if I saw it, I hoped to be able to explain it.

There was also a belief among some parents in the community that their children did just fine in school until they left the grade school and began junior high in Madras, where they were outnumbered by the Anglo children in their classes by a ratio of five to one. These parents believed the Indian children only began *then* to have trouble in school. I wanted to be able to compare the Anglo and Indian children just before they went into Madras, to be able to determine empirically whether there was a basis for the parents' belief.

Community Research

There were several important reasons for determining how both children and adults behaved in the community where the Indian children observed in school lived. First, if there were community-wide patterns in the use of language, they were likely to be fragmented in the classroom. Given the imposition of Anglo organization of interaction, an Anglo person controlling the interaction, and topical focus on Anglo substantive concerns, it seemed likely that expression which was culturally distinctive to the Indian children would be cut up, adumbrated, or displayed in bits and pieces in the classroom. I expected to see behavior that made no sense in the classroom be explained by seeing it occur in socially appropriate contexts in community settings.

In addition, one could not assume that the Indian children would behave in the same ways outside school as they did in school. Indian children might be behaving in a manner different from Anglo children because they were bored, confused, or fearful—that is, the cultural differences could result in the production of behavior that was not socially appropriate or desirable to either Anglos or Indians.

A second purpose in observing in the community was to determine how the Indian children came to be different from the Anglo children, or to determine how socialization in communicative skills was taking place.

The final reason for participating in community activities was to determine whether and in what ways adult behavior was similar to and different from that of the children. The adult behavior could reveal both the outcome or end product of the socialization, and the nature of adult models that constituted part of the socialization process for the children.

In sum, the study was distinguished by a four-way comparison

of Anglo and Indian first- and sixth-grade classrooms and by research in the Indian community to explain the behavior observed in
the classrooms.

In all of these contexts, the key method of data collection was
participant observation. Often the role was one of observer, for activities where such a role was considered culturally appropriate for a
non-Indian, as was true for classroom events, tribal business meetings known as general councils, and some social and religious
gatherings. In other contexts it was possible to become more actively
and directly involved with members of the community, or to be
more fully a participant. This was most possible in the homes of the
people I visited frequently or stayed with.

My source of information was the face-to-face interaction with
the members of the Warm Springs community. My attention was focused on the organization of that interaction. And, my analysis proceeded through comparing and contrasting the behavior in the
diverse contexts that I observed.

Part II

Communication in the Warm Springs Indian Community

3

The Warm Springs Indian Reservation

The purpose of this chapter is to offer a characterization of the Warm Springs Reservation that will provide the ethnographic context for the discussion of Warm Springs residents' culturally distinctive communicative behavior that follows. The reservation is in many ways both a geographical and a cultural isolate in relation to the non-Indian populations that surround it. The interactional network of most of the Warm Springs reservation Indians is almost entirely Indian. The ties that link them to Anglos may on occasion be numerous, but they are for the most part lacking in intensity or depth.

It is through Anglo-Indian contact that the Warm Springs Indians' sense of identity as "Indian" and not white is fed and maintained. But it is the largely Indian network of interaction that sustains the culturally distinctive ways of regulating communication in face-to-face interaction. In order to understand why and how the Warm Springs Reservation constitutes such a relatively bounded entity, it is necessary to know something about the history and current social organization of the reservation.

The Reservation as a Political and Social Unit

The Warm Springs Reservation is located in central Oregon, just east of the Cascade range. Its some 600,000 acres shade from mountain forests into a semiarid plateau that is crosscut by fast-running streams. Some of the streams drop down through canyons that provide sheltered locations for homes and for the main reservation town of Warm Springs in the southeastern part of the reservation. The approximately 2,000 tribal members live in the several neighborhoods that comprise the town of Warm Springs, or are scattered throughout the rural areas of the reservation.

The reservation was established in 1855, following the signing of a treaty at The Dalles on the Columbia River, for the purpose of gathering the Indians south of the Columbia River and east of the Cascades into a single location.

Federal policy for establishing reservations during this period dictated that they should be located in areas remote from Anglo settlement to protect the Indians from the destructive and corruptive influences of the whites (Coan, 1922). While this was the official justification for the isolation of Indian groups, there were other motives as well. Efforts were made to locate Indian populations in areas that not only were not presently occupied by Anglos, but also were not likely to become occupied by them. Effort was made to center reservations in areas that could not be farmed, and did not in other ways readily yield subsistence or income, i.e. areas that were barren.

Efforts were also made to locate reservations at some distance from one another, and to separate those Indians who were inclined to resist federal control by waging war against local Anglo populations. As Coan (1922) has noted, of all the reservations established in the Northwest during this period, the Warm Springs reservation best met the criteria established by federal policy makers. It was geographically isolated from Anglo settlement and the land was quite rocky and not easily irrigated.

In its relation to the federal government, Warm Springs is like other reservations in the United States. The government, and more specifically the Bureau of Indian Affairs (BIA), has legal obligations that involve both the reservation as a land base and as a people. Reservation land is held in trust by the federal government on behalf of the Indian people who are "enrolled in the tribe." Land within reservation boundaries is not subject to state property tax, and human activities that occur on reservation land are not subject to state laws. Such activities are, however, subject to federal laws, particularly those laws specifically enacted to regulate the affairs of enrolled tribal members when they are on the reservation. Resident tribal members are also subject to laws enacted by the local reservation government.

Tribal membership is determined by birth. Tribal enrollees are those descended from the groups whose purported leaders signed the Treaty of 1855. More specifically, one must be able to prove an ancestry that is at least one-fourth derived from those who were first listed as enrollees or later legally added to the rolls. Those who are legally enrolled as tribal members have specific legal rights associated with that membership. They have rights to the land, and through their tribal voting rights are able to participate in and benefit economically from decisions regarding the uses made of the land and its resources. They have the right to participate in all tribal and federal health, welfare, education, and housing programs that have been developed for tribal members.

The fact that only enrolled members have these rights and have them only in relation to the reservation in which they are enrolled contributes to a stable reservation population and to the viability of the reservation as a political and economic entity.

Anthropologists have typically viewed "the reservation" as an artificial form of social organization imposed on traditional indigenous forms, and consequently lacking any real political or social viability. The bulk of the anthropological literature on North American Indians has tended to ignore the role of the reservation in Indian life, and to concentrate on the analysis, and sometimes reconstruction, of indigenous Indian social organization. The tendency has been for anthropologists to assume that the Bureau of Indian Affairs runs the reservation. The Indian tribal members are viewed as powerless, lacking control over their own destinies, and as maintaining traditional forms of social organization that either have not been vested with much real authority since the reservation was established, or have been gutted of that authority.

Such a description accurately portrays the major portion of most reservations' histories. However, at Warm Springs, and probably on most other reservations as well, tribal members have become a part of that reservation system to the degree that their lives are regulated by the social, political, and economic institutions that constitute the reservation. And in practice, there is no other social unit that has as broad an impact on the daily lives of Warm Springs residents on the reservation.

The Warm Springs Indian Reservation *was* imposed on qualitatively very different forms of social organization. The groups that were settled on the reservation by no means constituted an indigenous political entity when taken together. The greatest number of Indians settled on the reservation were Sahaptin speakers of several hunting and gathering bands (Tenino, Tygh, Wy-am), who today call themselves "Warm Springs" Indians. They were identified by name on the basis of their winter village locations in the steep-sided valleys of the rivers running into the Columbia from the south. These people only gradually moved southward onto the reservation after the treaty was signed in 1855, and tended to scatter through the northern part of the reservation. Today, the northern population center of Simnasho, identifiable by its cluster of dwellings, is considered to be the area where the most traditional Sahaptin tribal members live.

Traditionalism is considered much more likely to be characteristic of descendents of the Sahaptin speakers, than of Indians from the other reservation groups. It is they who carry on traditional ways of worshipping, and their music, songs, and dances are the ones most in evidence at traditional ceremonies. The Sahaptin language is the only Indian language spoken on a day-to-day basis on the reservation, although it is only among those over forty that one frequently hears the language being spoken. Some adults under the age of forty can understand a great deal of Sahaptin, but do not speak it, in part because they feel they don't speak it well enough. Few of the school age children know more than a few words of any Indian language. This situation is changing now, however, as the language is reintroduced through the schools.

In addition to the Sahaptin speakers now known as "Warm Springs" Indians, there were also some speakers of Chinookan languages settled on the reservation at the time the treaty was signed who call themselves "Wasco" Indians. Chinookan languages were spoken along the Columbia River from the Pacific Ocean to as far east as the present day town of The Dalles. The chief subsistence activity of the Chinookan was salmon fishing. At the great Celilo Falls on the Columbia, formerly just east of The Dalles, the Chinookan villages controlled the trading network that brought goods down the Columbia from the eastern Plateau and western Plains areas, and up the Columbia from the Northwest Coast area. Unlike the nearby Sahaptin speakers, the Chinookan maintained close ties with the Northwest Coast, and they shared the class system and slave-holding features of social organization considered typical of the Northwest Coast.

In the 1830s, most of the Chinookan village populations were badly decimated by disease. Cook (1955) has estimated that as much as 90 percent of the population may have been eradicated by several epidemics that passed through the Columbia and Willamette river valleys during this period. Thus, while many of those settled on the Warm Springs Reservation came from the principal Chinookan village on the southern shore of the Columbia near the Celilo Falls, and have hence come to be called by the anglicized version of the village name, Wasco, others came from the decimated areas as far west down the Columbia as the Willamette River. Many of them settled along the river banks near the BIA agency, where the town of Warm Springs is now (French, 1961). They are today considered to be the group within the reservation that is most assimilated to the Anglo way of doing things. Most of those who have been successful in the business of cattle raising and who today occupy the positions within the tribal administration that involve tribal businesses are Wascos. D. French (1961) has suggested that the contemporary Wasco skills in economic affairs can be traced back to their indigenous specialization in trading. While there are a few old Wascos who can still speak Wasco Chinook, they do not have the opportunity to speak it on a daily basis, and the language is not spoken by members of the younger generations.

In the 1870s yet another group of Indians, the smallest, was located on the reservation. The Paiutes in southern Oregon had been gradually forced northward during the Indian wars that followed the settlement of California by non-Indians. Some of them were settled by the federal government in the southeastern part of the Warm Springs Reservation. Whereas the Wasco and Warm Springs were traditionally friendly neighbors, the major experience of both groups with the Paiutes was warfare. As a result of both the small size of the Paiute group and the negative attitudes toward them on the part of the other Indians on the reservation, the Paiutes have had relatively little impact on the culture of the reservation as a whole.

From the point of view of tribal members themselves, there are thus three interreservation ethnic groups that comprise the reservation population, and the labels Warm Springs, Wasco, and Paiute are used on some occasions in identifying older people and explaining their behavior and political loyalties. However, these three groups have been together on the reservation for over a hundred years now and in each generation there has been intermarriage among them. Many of the children of these marriages would probably say they were Warm Springs Indians, if asked.

In the early days of the reservation, the three distinct languages served to identify individuals with one group rather than another, although the common mastery of more than one Indian language facilitated intergroup communication. But this multilingual situation probably also contributed to the increasing use of English as a lingua franca, and hastened the disappearance of linguistically marked group identities. Today the labels Wasco, Warm Springs, and Paiute are applied primarily to those old enough to have known and spoken one Indian language or the other. The three groups are now referred to collectively in local contexts as "the tribe." And for those under forty, it is enrollment as a member of the Warm Springs Confederated Tribes and residence on the reservation that give one claim to identification with the now more salient political entity, the reservation.

Warm Springs as a Plateau Reservation

In the North American Indian culture area that anthropologists refer to as the Plateau, of which Warm Springs is a part, it is not at all unusual for a reservation population to be made up of small social groupings that traditionally used different languages. Both the Umatilla Reservation in eastern Oregon and the Yakima Reservation to the north, in Washington, are similar to Warm Springs in that respect, and in the use of English as a common language.

In the Plains and southwestern areas where the original tribal groupings were larger and more cohesive, tribal identity is more salient, partly because a reservation has so many of one type of people. Examples would include the Crow, the Blackfoot, the Papago, and the Hopi Reservations. The native languages are used more by younger people in the Plains and the Southwest than in the Plateau, in part because there was less reason to use English as a common language than in the Plateau region.

Warm Springs has a great deal in common with some other Plateau reservations and those commonalities are reflected in similar sociolinguistic patterns—i.e., in the social patterning of the use of the native languages and English. But Warm Springs is atypical of the Plateau in other respects.

Warm Springs is unique among reservations in the Plateau in that its land base is almost entirely intact. The Allotment Act passed by Congress in 1887 contributed significantly to the fragmentation of the land bases on other reservations (e.g., the Yakima and Umatilla Reservations). This act called for the allotment of 160 acres to each individual adult enrolled as a tribal member, and allowed for the sale of any lands left over after allotment. It also permitted these individual allotments to pass out of trust status after a five-year period, rendering the land taxable by the state and subject to sale by the individual Indian owners. In spite of earlier government efforts to establish reservations on land that was of little value to Anglo settlers, many such areas later came to be of value as the more desirable areas filled up and new agricultural techniques resulted in a redefinition of what lands could be cultivated. On reservations holding land that could be farmed, logged, or used for cattle grazing, the

Allotment Act created great pressures on the BIA to allot the land, sell off what was left, and pressure individual Indian owners to remove their land from trust status and sell it. Where this occurred, the land still held by reservations is typically a checkerboard of the least desirable lands. The individual allotments still held in trust now have many heirs descended from the original allottee. Lacking a large land base, or the capital to develop it, these joint owners usually lease the land to large-scale farmers and ranchers for a small fee (Stern & Boggs, 1971).

On reservations with this checkerboard pattern, Anglos have settled on the land they have managed to acquire. On some such reservations, like the Yakima Reservation, urban areas populated chiefly by Anglos have developed to provide the supportive services required by the agricultural businesses in the area, so that the Indians on the reservation are often heavily outnumbered by the Anglos.

Warm Springs has escaped this pattern. During the period of allotment, the rocky plateau land of the reservation was of little value, so that even though individual allotments were made, there was little pressure to sell the remaining land or to move the individual allotments out of trust status. Thus, only 1 percent of the original reservation land has been sold to non-Indians. Eighty-three percent of the original land base is under the control of the tribal government, and the remaining allotted land is still retained in trust status.

The Indian Reorganization Act of 1934 brought a halt to the allotment policy. It also provided reservation populations with the choice of self-government through reservation constitutions and bylaws, and the election of tribal councils to function as executive bodies. And finally, the act provided reservations with the option of incorporating so that they would be able to contract with businesses to provide services to reservations, as well as develop business enterprises of their own.

With its land base intact, a functioning tribal government, and the business acumen of the Wasco, the Warm Springs Confederated Tribes were in a position to exploit their own resources. They had an additional advantage over other Indian populations in the area, namely a tribal unity apparently lacking on other reservations. This unity is most strikingly illustrated by the tribe's handling of funds awarded them by the federal government for loss of fishing rights along the Columbia River in 1958. Whereas the populations of other reservations voted to divide their compensatory funds among all individual members of the tribe, Warm Springs enrollees voted to devote the major portion of their $4 million to investment in tribal business enterprises. They invested $1.2 million in a small resort complex called Kah-nee-tah and have since then added a much larger convention center. In the 1960s, they were also able to obtain outside capital for the purchase and expansion of a saw mill for the processing of tribally owned timber that has increased in value as the Coastal Mountain timber sources have been depleted.

The tribal income from the stumpage (i.e., the cut timber) and from the saw mill operations has enabled the tribe to develop a number of tribal programs intended to be of benefit to the entire reservation population. The tribal bureaucracy that has developed to administer these programs is accordingly much larger than tribal bureaucracies on reservations of comparative size. A portion of the income is given out to individual enrolled members, and referred to as their "per capita payments." Each enrolled adult receives $60 a month. Each child receives $45, part of which is set aside in a trust fund that becomes available after the child becomes 18. The various tribal enterprises also provide jobs for reservation residents, and priority is given to tribal members in hiring. As a result of all this, the Warm Springs tribal members are among the more prosperous Indians in the country, although the credit-spending patterns of many still resemble those of the more impoverished sectors of our population.

This economic prosperity has also contributed to tribal political cohesiveness. On other reservations in the Plateau many tribal members have left, usually because they have been unable to earn a living on the reservation. This in turn has often resulted in a political split between enrolled members who live off the reservation and those who live on the reservation, particularly when decisions must be made regarding the allocation of funds. When enrolled members must decide what to do with tribal income, and monetary compensations awarded by the federal government for claims made against it for treaty violations, the off-reservation members are more likely to press for distribution of such funds to individuals. On-reservation members are more likely to argue for the investment of such funds in tribal programs because they are in a better position to benefit from such programs.[1] Because Warm Springs tribal members are able to obtain employment on the reservation, over 90 percent of the enrollees are now living on the reservation, and thus share a concern to handle tribal funds in ways that will benefit those living on the reservation.

To summarize the characterization of the Warm Springs Reservation thus far, we find that Warm Springs is similar to other reservations in the area in its most essential features as a legal entity with direct political ties to the federal government, but fewer ties with state- or local-level political entities. Like other reservations in the Plateau area, Warm Springs was originally made up of small band and village units whose group identities have partially merged into a reservation identity. Warm Springs differs from other reservations in the Plateau in the extent to which its land base has remained intact, the relative absence of Anglo economic, social, and political institutions on the reservation,[2] the relative lack of political factionalism, and the availability of natural resources that the tribe has been in a position to develop. All of the features that distinguish the Warm Springs Reservation have contributed to the strengthening of the reservation as a viable political unit.

The Internal Organization of the Reservation

Since the Indian Reorganization Act of 1935, and the attendant efforts of the BIA to encourage the development of tribal governments, reservations have varied in the extent to which such governments have been supported by tribal members. They also vary in the extent to which they have been run by tribal members rather than by BIA bureaucrats assigned to reservations and area offices. The BIA bureaucracy has survived at Warm Springs, but the official "line" is that BIA employees function solely in an advisory capacity to the tribal government. This official view is in keeping with appearances. The superintendent of the reservation is typically present but silent at political meetings. At the same time, the tribe is dependent on the expertise of federal advisors in the management of their business enterprises, and still very much subject to federal policy in Indian affairs. Nevertheless, compared to other reservations, the tribal government at Warm Springs does in practice exercise greater control over tribal affairs than many other reservation governments.

The Tribal Council is the body responsible for governing tribal affairs. Three of the Tribal Council members are identified as the "chiefs" of the Warm Springs, Wasco, and Paiute groups. They are permanent members of the council once they have been selected by each of those groups through popular vote (among Wasco) or inheritance of the position (among Warm Springs and Paiute). The reservation is divided into districts originally apportioned to be equal in population, and each district elects its own representatives to the council.

Elections are held for all positions once every three years, and at each election a third to half of the seven elected councilmen are new to the council. The chairman of the council is then elected by the council. One traditional form of social organization that is important in election policies is the Long House religion, a contemporary derivative of the Prophet Cult (DuBois, 1938), best known to anthropologists for its contribution to the Ghost Dance of the 1890s. The long house religion, also known as "washat," "worship dance," and "the old people's way of worshipping," is visibly present in the form of the long houses themselves—the buildings in which the traditional ritual activities take place. There are long houses in both the town of Warm Springs and the cluster of dwellings called Simnasho in the northern part of the reservation. A third long house is used by members of both long houses. Each of the town long houses has several old people who are identified as long house leaders associated with it. They assume responsibility for people organized to carry out various ritual and social activities, and for regulating ritual activity that occurs.

Tribal members who participate in long house activities are affiliated with either one long house or the other, but not both, even though they may take part in the activities that are sponsored by both. Long house affiliation could be said to be inherited, in that one typically becomes involved with the long house of the parent who has been the most active participant in the religion, usually the mother.

Long house affiliation is reflected through involvement in certain aspects of the activity required to carry out long house affairs. The most prominent of these affairs are the Root Feast in the spring and the Huckleberry Feast in the late summer. Both of these feasts entail the ritual serving of certain foods just as they reach the harvestable stage, preceded by the drumming, singing, and dancing to Worship Dance songs. Each celebration requires personnel to amass, prepare, and serve large quantities of food, and to carry out the worship dancing. Those who engage in such activities are typically affiliated with the specific long house organization through which the activity is carried out. The long house is also responsible for carrying out the extensive ritual activities surrounding the death of its members—activities which typically involve the extended kin of both the deceased and the spouse.[3] And finally, the naming ceremonies through which children are given Indian names are usually held in conjunction with ritual activities of the long house with which the family of the children being named is affiliated.

The work involved in maintaining the community and individual ritual cycles brings long house members into frequent interaction with one another, and reinforces the kinship ties among them.

Their talk on such occasions often turns to the political activities of the Tribal Council. During the period of my research, the leaders of the Simnasho Longhouse took a particularly strong interest in the political process, and were always present for and active in the frequent General Council meetings where council members discuss their doings with the community at large. In the months before a Tribal Council election, there is much discussion of who would make a good council member and who would not, and there is a close correlation between those well spoken of and those elected. There is evidence, then, that the long house networks play an active role in shaping the political process, particularly through their advocation of particular individuals for key positions in the tribal government. Long house leaders do not themselves run for office or actively seek central positions in the tribal bureaucracy. The contemporary and traditional spheres of authority are thus kept separate structurally, but the traditional leadership nevertheless has considerable influence on the political structures in which they do not occupy positions.

Those who are nominated for and elected to council positions are usually men in their late forties to mid-sixties whose families participate in long house affairs, and who have a source of income that enables them to devote a great deal of time to tribal affairs for relatively little financial recompense. The tradition of allocating authority to "the old people" of the reservation on the grounds that they are wiser or more knowledgeable than the young people, and hence worthy of respect, is still quite strong at Warm Springs. Yet at the same time, the old people frequently complain that the young adults do not take a sufficiently active interest in reservation politics. The old people also express the opinion that the future of the reservation will depend on the skills acquired by the young adults through the many tribally funded educational programs that receive strong support from the old people. Some of the younger adults, however, say that when they do attempt to become involved they are rebuffed. But with the rapidly growing population on the reservation (the average number of children per family is five), and a lopsided demographic profile in which more than half the population is under 16, the influence of the young adults has inevitably increased. Thus, in the tribal election of 1971, a council member under 35 years of age was elected for the first time from the district in which the town of Warm Springs is located, where the younger and more acculturated portion of the population is concentrated, and other young adults have come onto the council since then.

It is the responsibility of the Tribal Council to oversee the functioning of the Tribal Administration, whose employees are held directly accountable to the Tribal Council. The head of the Tribal Administration, known as the general manager of the reservation, is appointed by the Tribal Council. The general manager in turn hires and oversees the work of a number of department heads such as the education department, the police, purchasing, maintenance, and forest production industries. The position of general manager is probably the single most powerful position on the reservation, for a number of reasons. The general manager, like the department heads under him, occupies his position over a number of years, devotes full time to his work, and comes to acquire detailed and specialized knowledge of the functioning of the tribal businesses and programs. He is college educated, as are an increasing number of department heads, and is younger and more acculturated than the Tribal Council members. The council members, by contrast, do not usually have long-term tenure in their offices and they are not in a position financially to devote all of their time to their political duties. Consequently, they do not acquire the same degree of specialized expertise in tribal affairs that administration employees do. Because of this, council members must rely on the knowledge, sincerity, and honesty of the tribal administration employees in making their decisions. Yet both the council and the population that elects them are aware of the danger that the authority most tribal members believe should be vested in the council can easily shift to the administration, and particularly to the general manager. It is fair to say that everyone watches the council quite closely, while the council in turn is expected to watch the administration quite closely.

Both political and economic links to the world outside the reservation are maintained primarily through council and administration personnel, particularly the Tribal Council chairman and the general manager. They are the ones who most often deal with the federal bureaucracy; they are the ones who contract with the universities, businesses, and legal firms that provide the "expert" advise on which the reservation government relies in maintaining its tribal businesses and in developing plans for the future. Otherwise, the links between the reservation population and the Anglo world outside the reservation are few and for the most part rather brief and impersonal.

Local Indian-Anglo Relations

Most face-to-face interaction between Warm Springs Indians and Anglos occurs in the off-reservation town of Madras (population c2,500), 15 miles from the reservation's eastern border. There are few commercial enterprises on the reservation, so people from Warm Springs usually go to Madras to buy food, shop for clothes and household items, eat at restaurants, drink at the bars, and take advantage of the bowling alley and movie theaters that offer public entertainment. Tribal members also travel less frequently to more distant but larger cities like The Dalles, Bend, and Portland to carry out major economic transactions (e.g., to purchase a car, furniture, appliances) and to obtain hospital care that is not available at either the Public Health Service clinic on the reservation or at the hospital in Madras.

Most of the encounters between Indian and Anglo in Madras, then, occur in public places, entail economic transactions, and are relatively ritualized and anonymous in character. Very rarely do Indians go to the homes of people in Madras. People from Warm Springs tell of encounters with Anglos in Madras that suggest the demeaning treatment they receive in such situations—stories about being watched in stores as if they were potential thieves, being refused service in restaurants, being unfairly arrested, and most often, stories about being ignored and treated as strangers by Anglos they have come to know personally in a less public circumstance (e.g., in a job situation, as a visitor under special circumstances on the reservation, in school).

The Indians are clearly looked down upon by some of the Madras townspeople and treated disdainfully by them. However, most Warm Springs residents still have some good relationships with Anglos in the town of Madras.

The Anglo-Indian contact, replete as it is with cultural sources of miscommunication, functions in such a way as to crystallize and reinforce the ethnic identity of "Indian," for both Warm Springs Indians and the Anglos with whom they come into contact. The Anglo people who live in Madras come to associate certain ways of interacting with a certain physical type and dress; together these are taken as Indian. Indians similarly come to expect certain behaviors of Anglo people.

The Anglo stereotype of the Indian is, however, primarily a local phenomenon. It exists primarily in the Anglo towns on or just off reservations all over the country. In areas where there is no large Indian population, or where Indian homes are widely scattered, no such stereotype exists. Until the recent media publicity on reservation conditions and on the activities of the American Indian Movement, the majority of the U.S. population was not even aware that Indians still existed in this country. For the Indian, however, his selfidentification as an Indian, and his identification of Anglos as non-Indian is always with him. Thus, Warm Springs Indians who have lived in large urban areas like Portland have expressed their surprise at being treated "as an individual," or "just like anybody else." They are even more surprised to meet people who refuse to believe them when they say they are Indians.

The public places of Madras, then, provide the main contexts in which face-to-face interaction between adult Warm Springs Indians and the surrounding white population occurs. These public encounters can thus be said to constitute and the boundary areas through which the two ethnic groups come into contact with one another, and in Barth's terms (1969), they are also the encounters that maintain the boundaries between the two groups, reinforcing as they do ethnic stereotypes, and the mutual awareness of a lack of cultural commonality.

But it is probably through their school experiences that Warm Springs children have their most extensive and prolonged contact with Anglo ways of organizing interaction. It is also in the classroom that the power differential between Indian and Anglos is probably greatest, given that it is reinforced by the authority of adult over child.

For several decades in the early part of this century, children from Warm Springs attended and lived in the BIA boarding school established on the reservation. The BIA boarding school was an institution designed to eradicate the Indian culture the children had learned in their first six years at home. At the same time, the school maintained the children in interactional isolation from the Anglo world to which they were supposed to become assimilated. Today, all of the children from Warm Springs attend a grade school on the reservation that is part of a local district of the state school system. Since reservation land is not taxed by the state, federal funds are usually provided for children attending state schools. But in this case, the Warm Springs tribal government pays tribal monies into a federal fund established for this purpose. Roughly 95 percent of the children attending the Warm Springs school are Indian, although all of their teachers were white at the time of my study. At the end of their first six grades, the children are bussed into Madras where they are outnumbered by Anglo students by a ratio of five to one. There, in the junior high and high schools, the Indian students are by and large socially segregated from the Anglo students by mutual preference, even though they attend classes together. When friendships do develop across ethnic lines, the students still rarely visit one another in their homes, although they may spend time together cruising the rural areas in their cars. And even these friendships only rarely continue after the friends have completed school. It is primarily through their contact with Anglo teachers, administrators, and other school employees, then, that the children come into direct contact with mainstream Anglo culture.

People from Madras rarely go out to the Warm Springs Reservation. When they do, it is usually as guests of the tribal government. Nor are the residents of Madras the exception. While many outsiders pass through the reservation to other places, few find reason or means to stay for any length of time.

A comparison of Madras and the *town* of Warm Springs reveals some of the reasons why the segregation of Anglo and Indian continues. In the town of Warm Springs, there are actually two levels or types of "public" sphere. One of these is comparable to the public sphere of Madras. It consists of those facilities open to the general public, and marked as being such by the type of building, building facade, and signs that all of us use in identifying the functions of public places. But these are few in number. On the main highway that runs through the reservation, there are two restaurants and two gas stations within reservation boundaries.

Unlike Madras, the town of Warm Springs has a second public sphere, one that is essentially public only to tribal members. It consists of the tribal office buildings, the Public Health Service Clinic, the community center, and the longhouse. These are freely open to tribal members, but because the services they offer are legally for tribal members and their families specifically, few people from off the reservation have cause to use them. A combined general store and post office, and several churches in the town are theoretically open to the general public. However, the town is not layed out in the familiar Western grid pattern, and there are few if any signs pointing the way for outsiders to find these facilities, let alone make use of them. The community is organized in a way that presumes or presupposes knowledge of its spatial and social organization.

But there are other aspects of reservation community life that discourage outsiders from taking part in community life as well. Whereas it is possible for new people to move into a town like Madras, either because they have obtained a job there or because they like the area, it is quite difficult for new people to move onto the reservation. Priority in job hiring is given to tribal members. Information about jobs typically is spread by word of mouth. Housing is difficult to obtain. In a situation of chronic housing shortage, those who own land and houses usually make any extra space they have available to kinsmen. Tribally controlled housing is allocated primarily to tribal employees. And again, information about available housing is spread by word of mouth. Occasionally people who have no kin ties with reservation residents do move onto the reservation, but they rarely stay for long. Anglo tribal employees who have been provided with housing by the tribal members find it difficult to become involved in the social network of the reservation. The social life of the Indians is primarily with their kinsmen; even those who have been neighbors for years are more likely to see more of their relatives than one another. Those who say that "everybody is related to everybody else" on the reservation come close to the truth. Everyone knows almost everyone else's name and kinship ties, and those who don't know can readily be located by reference to the name of a primary kinsman.

For all these reasons, the interactional network of Warm Springs Indians is largely Indian. If one accompanies the adult members of an Indian family in their routine activities, it is possible to go for long periods of time each day without engaging in interaction with an Anglo person, and then only across a counter where money is being exchanged. Because of this primarily Indian network of interaction a culturally distinctive social milieu has been maintained and has facilitated culturally different ways of communicating.

Notes

1. Stern and Boggs (1971) illustrate this pattern for the Umatilla Reservation in Eastern Oregon in detail.

2. The work of Stern and Boggs (1971) suggests that the presence of Anglo economic activity on reservations has been an important factor in the relatively disorganized state of many reservation populations and their governments. At Umatilla, for example, the relation between Indian landlords and their Anglo farmer tenants has assumed many of the social functions once accomplished through kinship ties. Thus a tenant will provide winter firewood for the landlord, or aid him in tilling his garden as a way of maintaining good relations and assuring the continuation of his lease. At Warm Springs, many such services formerly exchanged by kinsmen are now carried out by the tribal government, having been absorbed by various tribal programs.

3. Longhouse activities are discussed in more detail in French (1955) and Philips (1975b).

4

The Use of the Auditory and Visual Channels of Communication among Warm Springs Indians

Introduction

One basic thesis of this book is that Warm Springs Indian children begin school with a background that is culturally somewhat different from the background presumed by and built upon in school curricula. More particularly, Indian children have already acquired culturally distinctive ways of communicating or conveying information that are different from the teachers' ways of conveying information. Moreover, those differences contribute to miscommunication between teacher and student.

Chapter 3 describes features of Warm Springs social organization that contribute to the maintenance of a largely Indian network of relationships for most of the residents of Warm Springs. From this network we infer that Warm Springs children spend most of the time before they enter school with other Indians. This constant interaction with other Indians during those first six years when children learn so much provides the basis for the continuation of a distinctly Indian way of life.

This chapter describes and analyzes the Indian adult patterns of communication that provide the models of appropriate communicative behavior for the children.

The organization of Chapter 4 draws upon the comparative framework developed in Part I of this book, where attention focused on the cross-cultural similarities and differences in the communicative functions of the auditory and visual channels in conveying attention. In the discussion to follow, I will first provide a general characterization of the relative functions of the visual and auditory channels in both the daily work life and the public social activities of Warm Springs residents. Then attention will focus in greater detail on the relative roles of verbal and nonverbal behavior in the structuring of attention in Warm Springs interaction.

Verbal and nonverbal modes of communication typically fulfill very different functions because of the quite different ways in which messages are organized and processed. However, in the important activity of accomplishing and conveying mutual attention between speaker and hearer, there is an overlap in function of the visual and auditory channels. Consequently, the possibility of cultural variability in both channel and form of message used in securing and conveying attention arises. And as will become apparent, cultural differences in the structuring of attention can be an important source of miscommunication when persons of different cultural backgrounds interact with one another.

Channel choices and combinations made by the people of Warm Springs in organizing communication in face-to-face interaction differ from those of the mainstream culture of white middle class Americans.

One of the most salient features of Warm Springs communication in face-to-face interaction is that there is more of it than there is among Anglos. People generally spend more time with others, and accordingly, less time alone. Even activities for which only one person is necessary, or that can only be accomplished by one person (e.g., cashing a check, or getting a driver's license) are usually done in the company of another. Very few people live alone, and even those who do spend a great deal of time staying with others.

Much of the talk that occurs between tribal members is done in conjunction with physical activity. People often simply sit and "visit" (i.e., talk) with one another. However, when compared with middle-class Anglos, a much larger proportion of their talk is accompanied by a greater amount of physical activity, usually in the form of work. For some of this activity, it is more the joint work that influences the organization of interaction, with talk being interspersed as it is convenient, as when women are digging for roots or cooking, or men are riding for horses or repairing a car. On other occasions, the talk itself is given priority, and the tasks that accompany it are individual rather than coordinated, as when a man repairs a harness, or a woman does beadwork. In general, then, there is more information being processed in both channels in Warm Springs face-to-face interaction a larger proportion of the time than is true of Anglo middle-class interaction.

There are a number of features of Warm Springs life that contribute to the commonness of combined physical and linguistic activity. First, many people at Warm Springs live a rural life, even in the town of Warm Springs. They hunt, they fish, and they process the food from these activities. They keep and use domesticated animals. They drive long distances to reach necessary services. To sustain such a life it is necessary to engage in a greater amount of physical activity than is true of urban dwellers. However, all of these activities are characteristic of non-Indian dwellers in rural areas as well.

In addition, from a societal point of view, Warm Springs Indians share many of the attributes of non-Indian members of the working class. Their occupational activity involves more physical labor. Most of the men work at the saw mill, or are hired by the tribe to do construction and maintenance work for the reservation. The women are hired by the tribal industries and the tribal government as waitresses, maids, day care center and Head Start aids, typists and clerks Some are hired by an electronics corporation to wind wires around tiny components through a magnifying glass. With the exception of typing, these jobs entail lesser amounts of sitting, talking, and writing than do the so-called white-collar jobs associated with the middle class.[1]

Like other segments of the working class, Warm Springs people supplement their smaller incomes with their own labor during the periods of time when they are not engaged in work for pay. They do things middle-class people hire others to do. They spend more time attempting to repair and expand their own houses. They also spend more time attempting to repair their cars, although older Indians do less of this than older Anglo working-class men.

Tribal members buy cheaper foods that require more processing time. They supplement their purchased food with hunting and fishing, berry picking, and canning fruits purchased in wholesale lots. Some tribal members work along with migrants laborers in harvesting seasonal crops in the area.

Indian women supplement income with other forms of labor less common to non-Indian working-class people, particularly the women over thirty who still have traditional skills. They are hired by young Indian men to make beaded buckskin war-dancing outfits, and they sell buckskin and beadwork to the local store in the town of Warm Springs. They dig roots and bulbs, and preserve them by grinding and drying the roots and by smoking the bulbs. Once again,

those activities require physical involvement. Physical activity consequently consumes a larger proportion of the time of lower- or working-class people, Indian and non-Indian alike.

People help one another in the activities that supplement labor.
They share the fruits of such labor when they hunt, fish, and gather
wild foods. They also give food away to other kinsmen, and house
them. The majority of reciprocal labor is done among kinsmen, and
usually among members of one's extended family, but the people
who help one another are sometimes more distantly related, or just
friends.

It is difficult to compare the labor reciprocality of Indian and
non-Indian working-class groups. It seems likely that among Anglo
working-class people such activities are done together more among
age-group peers, fewer of whom will be kinsmen, and that when
non-Indian lower-class members see their kinsmen, more of the time
spent together will be in visiting—i.e., talking. It also seems likely
that there is less food sharing or boarding of anybody, let alone kinsmen, among Anglo working-class people. And finally, it seems likely that the overall amount of time that Indians spend working in the
companionship of others, rather than alone, is probably greater.

In the public life of the community, where activities involve
large numbers of people and interaction is structured and predict-
able, or ritualized, there is evidence of a specialization of function
for communication in both the visual and auditory channels.

Relatively pure talk that does not entail physical labor handled
in the visual channel is used in business and political meetings
through which decisions are made about the allocation of tribal
funds and the organization of tribal programs. While there are many
such meetings, those most open to the public are the General Council meetings where members of the Tribal Council and Administration discuss their activities with the whole community.

In the ritual activities of the long house religion and the Shaker
Church,[2] by contrast, roughly equal weight is given to the visual
and auditory channels in the organization of ritual interaction.
However, by comparison with the ritual activities that occur within
the framework of Anglo Christian churches, a much larger proportion of Warm Springs ritual is organized through the visual channel.

In general, such ritual activity can be characterized in terms of
an alternation between ritual interaction in which the visual channel
is dominant and ritual interaction in which the auditory channel is
dominant, although the two are sometimes combined. Thus the
worship dance activities carried out in the long houses usually alter-

nate between singing and dancing the worship dance itself and short testimonial or exhortative speeches given by individuals.

In a third set of large-scale public events, interaction is organized almost completely through physical activity conveyed in the visual channel. As a group, such events could be characterized as fulfilling the functions of entertainment and artistic expression. Included in this category would be Indian social dancing—also referred to generically as war dancing—Indian gambling, and western-derived rodeos and sporting events.

When the distribution of use of the auditory and visual channels in large-scale public events is considered in general, one aspect of its patterning is quite obvious: use of the auditory channel prevails in circumstances where the transmission of information is an important function of the activity, as in the talk at the various political meetings held on the reservation. Use of the visual channel prevails in highly ritualized activities where the transmission of new information is relatively unimportant. It is difficult to see how it could be otherwise. Language is distinguished by its inherent capacity for the transmission of highly discrete and unique messages, especially when compared with the redundant and nondiscrete quality of non-verbal information.

A second type of patterning in the use of the auditory and visual channels emerges when we consider *who* it is within the community that participates in interactions that constitute the focus of attention for those who participate as members of the audience. Almost without exception, those who fulfill the speaking roles are over 35 while those who fulfill the roles requiring physical activity are under 35, and usually under 30. Thus at General Council meetings, those who run the meetings and those who verbally raise issues of relevance to the whole tribe are older. Similarly, those who at long house events testify, make speeches, and name the foods are usually old people. The drummer singers for all forms of dancing are usually older, and younger men will defer to the older men prepared to assume this role. By contrast, the athletes, the rodeo competitors, the worship dancers and war dancers are usually young people. But people of all ages do join the general social dancing, and those who participate in Indian gambling include adults of various ages.

In general, however, there is a pattern of specialization in physical activity in the visual channel for young people, and specialization in verbal skills in the auditory channel for older people. Since it is through the auditory channel that new information is transmitted, and older people are thought to have greater knowledge by virtue of their age, it is again understandable that such a pattern emerges.

One factor affecting participation is the existence of performance standards that should be met if one is to participate in public events in a manner that will be the focus of attention of many. Application of evaluative criteria to such activities affect who actually participates. For physical activities, *control* of the body is probably the aspect of behavior given most evaluative attention, rather than, say, strength, speed, grace, or individual distinctiveness of movement. Thus the war dancers in competition are evaluated on the basis of their ability to change rhythmic dance patterns as the rhythmic pattern of the drum changes, to maintain balance while the weight is on one foot and the other foot weaves a pattern in the air, to bend the knees without loss of stability, and to stop without wavering when the music stops. And physical control is obviously a skill of the young, among non-Indians as well as Indians.

In verbal presentations, value is placed on economy of speech, control (e.g., the absence of false starts, the appearance of calmness), and probably most important, evidence that knowledge and forethought have been given to what is discussed. Many Warm Springs Indians hold that it takes many years to acquire these verbal skills. Thus, however fluent a young person may be in conversation, he is likely to lack the confidence to come forward to speak at a large public event, and to feel that were he to do so he would be viewed as audacious, and as assuming more skill and knowledge than he in fact could have. Some young adults who did come forward at public meetings during the period of my research later expressed in private their nervousness and their feeling of a lack of support, or even indifference, for what they had to say.

The allocation of physical specializations to younger people and verbal specializations to older people does not differentiate Warm Springs Indians from Anglos in a general way. In general, Anglo allocation of communicative skills and roles follows a similar pattern. Indeed, the pattern should be widespread cross-culturally because members of the human species generally tend to mature and peak physically before they do so verbally.

Even so, there is still a difference in emphasis between Anglo and Indian orientation toward visual and auditory skills. A greater proportion of the population of teenagers and young adults of Warm Springs is drawn into public activities requiring the demonstration of physical skills than in Anglo communities. And a smaller proportion of that same young Indian group is drawn into public verbal activity than in Anglo communities. Here the cultural process pushes and shapes the developmental process to give it a particular emphasis.

The allocation of visual and verbal activities in the Warm Springs community results in the overall impression that greater use is made of the visual channel among Indians than among Anglos.

Yet when a direct comparison is made between Indian and Anglo interaction that is structured primarily through talk, a different impression is conveyed.

The Attention Structure of Warm Springs Interaction

Interaction Structured through Talk

As should be apparent from the discussion of social life at Warm Springs, activities vary in the extent to which they are structured through physical activity or through talk. And there are other properties of interaction that are related to the degree to which interaction is structured through talk.

First of all, as Part I of this book suggests, interaction structured through talk by no means excludes the use of the visual channel. Those within speaking range are always within seeing range (although barriers can impede access). And because of the distinctive properties of the visual and auditory channel, successful transmission of linguistic messages is facilitated by the use of the visual channel.

We use the visual channel to obtain information conveyed by facial expression and gesture, most of which could be characterized as emotional or affective. But we can also use the visual channel to convey attention and to determine whether others are paying attention to us. In other words, we use the visual channel as well as the auditory channel to *structure attention*.

Where physical activity conveyed in the visual channel creates structure, information is continuously sent and received by parties to the interaction. By contrast, where talk structures the interaction, those engaged in interaction take turns sending messages, and alternate between the positions of speaker and hearer. And every time there is a speaker change, the attention structure is renegotiated.

In the remaining section of this chapter discussion will focus on the ways in which Warm Springs Indians' structuring of attention in interaction organized through talk is culturally different from that of Anglos. As we will see, Warm Springs residents differ in the ways in which they use both the auditory and visual channels in conveying attention and determining whether others are paying attention to them. Such differences in turn affect the ways in which the attention structure is renegotiated when speaker change occurs, affect how one "gets the floor."

The Structure of Attention

In Part I, I discussed the conditions that must be met in order for a verbal message to be successfully transmitted. First a speaker must attract the attention of a listener, and in so doing convey whose attention is sought. Second, the prospective listener must recognize or perceive that the speaker is seeking the listener's attention. Third, the listener must convey attention to the speaker, or let the speaker know that the listener is attending. Finally the speaker must recognize or perceive that a listener is paying attention.

The communicative competence involved in structuring attention is, then, both productive and receptive. The speaker produces behavior that attracts attention and receives behavior from the hearer that conveys attention. Relatedly, the hearer produces behavior that conveys attention to the speaker and receives behavior that attracts attention and designates the hearer as the person being addressed. As we will see, the people of Warm Springs meet those conditions in culturally distinctive ways.

A speaker may attract the attention of a listener using either the visual or the auditory channel. In the *visual* channel, the speaker attracts attention through speaker-specific facial movements and gestures. Gestures in particular may catch the eye of those within range and enable them to determine who it is that is speaking. Indians of Warm Springs differ from Anglos in speaker-specific body movements in several ways. In general there is less speaker-specific body movement by Indian speakers than by Anglo speakers. There is less bobbing of the head in rhythm with the speech, less shifting from one position to another at topical junctures in speech, and less hand gesturing by Indian speakers. The hand gestures that are used in conjunction with speech are for the most part closer to the body than in Anglo speech and tend to sweep vertically rather than horizontally where a point is emphasized. Thus Indian speakers sometimes give the impression of taking up less space and being more self-contained than Anglo speakers.

The form of the hand gestures is also qualitatively distinctive, in that the fingers of the hand are positioned somewhat differently in relation to one another, although it is difficult to characterize that difference more precisely. The same forms of hand gestures have quite stylized varients in the gesturing that accompanies the telling of myths by old people and in the signalling used in bone gambling.

The facial movements that accompany speech by Warm Springs Indians are also somewhat different from the facial movements of Anglo speakers. The general impression supported by videotaped recordings of interaction is that there is less movement in the lower part of the face and more movement in the area around the eyes.

Thus far I have spoken only of the speaker's behavior in the *visual* channel that may attract the attention of potential listeners and aid them in locating and identifying the speaker. In addition to the behavior that generally attracts attention, there is also speaker behavior that conveys more precisely who it is that the speaker is trying to attract. A speaker may not wish all of those within hearing to attend, and so may behave in such a way as to *designate an addressed recipient*.

It is common to determine whose attention a speaker is seeking by the alignment and gaze direction of the speaker. Speakers in many cultures tend to face those they are addressing and to gaze in their direction, presumably to see if they are returning the gaze and are in fact paying attention. Often Anglo speakers designate and identify their addressed recipients by facing them more directly than others they are facing, and by gazing in their faces more often than they gaze at others.

Warm Springs speakers also face those they are speaking to or addressing. But they do not gaze into the faces of those they face as much as Anglos do, and they do not as often gaze at certain individuals more than at others. Instead, the gaze of the speaker is directed more equally toward those the speaker is facing. This does not mean that Indian speakers never focus their gaze on certain individuals more often than others, but rather that less of their speech is directed in this way.

Thus far I have discussed only the signaling in the *visual* channel that speakers use to attract attention and designate their listeners. Yet while the actions in the visual channel may help the listener locate and identify the speaker, signaling in the *auditory channel* is by definition the crucial attraction of a speaker. Speech itself attracts the attention of listeners because we assume that speech is intentional and toward some other person. But while speech serves this function among both Anglos and Warm Springs Indians, the quality of the speech is culturally distinctive for each group.

In most ordinary daily encounters Warm Springs people do not talk as loud as Anglos do, and they speak at a slightly slower pace with fewer occurrences of false starts and rephrasings. In addition, people at Warm Springs do not use changes or variation in voice loudness to attract attention in the ways that Anglos do. They do not talk louder and louder to attract the attention of those not alerted to a softer voice, or to give emphasis to some utterances, or to convey degrees of anger. In general the spatial range over which the voice is used to attract attention is smaller, and the spatial range over which signaling in the visual channel is used to attract attention is greater.

There are other differences in voice quality that enable some Indians and Anglos to say that they can tell whether a speaker is Indian or Anglo without seeing that person. These qualities are, however, difficult to describe and difficult to distinguish from pronunciation or phonological differences.

While use of the auditory channel to attract listeners is a simple matter, the verbal designation of listeners, or of who it is that is being addressed is more varied and complex. There are a number of ways in which a speaker may identify the person to whom the speech is addressed. The most obvious of these in English is to identify one's addressee by name, as in "Bill, what are you doing?" In addition, a speaker may speak in such a way that only some of those who are listening are in a position to fully understand and respond to what is said. This can be done in a variety of ways. Thus a speaker may say, "Do you remember the waitress at the place where we had lunch?" Clearly such an utterance is not addressed to those who do not know where the speaker had lunch. Similarly, if a speaker says, "I think the beginning of the Neolithic should be pushed back," those who know what the Neolithic is are in a better position to respond in a socially appropriate manner. At the same time, the type of shared knowledge drawn on by the speaker in implicitly designating possible respondents is qualitatively different in the two examples.

Warm Springs Indians less often use verbal means to designate specific individual listeners than Anglos do, just as they less often visually identify specific listeners. Address is more often general, so that the speaker appears to include all those present and facing one another as listeners.

In general, then, there are culturally distinctive ways in which Warm Springs speakers meet the first condition for the successful transmission of a verbal message—i.e., *attracting the attention of and designating or identifying listeners.*

The second condition that must be met for the successful transmission of a linguistic message is that the hearer must *recognize the attention-getting and designating activity of the speaker* for what it is. Thus meeting the second condition entails receptive competence on the part of the hearer, rather than productive competence of the speaker.

I have indicated that Warm Springs speakers' attention-getting behavior in both the visual and auditory channel is more subtle than that of Anglo speakers: speaker-specific movements are not as exaggerated and speech is not so loud. This suggests that if potential Indian hearers are to recognize that their attention is sought, or to receive that information, they need to be perceptually oriented to signaling of less intensity than Anglo hearers.

Visual attention to physical detail is evident in several ways. First both adults and children engage in long distance scanning, even when engaged in talk, and are more practiced than Anglos in the discrimination of movement and the identification of objects and persons at greater distances. Thus in highway travel, friends and relatives cars will be identified a quarter of a mile away. At rodeos relatives and friends on the opposite side of the corral performing area can and will be picked out from the crowd. And at distances of half a mile to two miles, the mountainside movement of horses and persons are casually pointed out, and the horses' identification and ownership noted.

This emphasis on attention to physical detail is also apparent in more formalized aspects of traditional Indian culture, some of which are no longer manifested in day-to-day life on the reservation. The most obvious example is the well-known vision quest through which young Indians attained the support and protection or "power" of supernatural spirits. In this quest, it was a visually received manifestation of a spirit that provided the centrally validating evidence that the questor was indeed the recipient of this power. But more relevantly here, visually received evidence was also the central source of community validation of the vision. The questor was forbidden to provide a verbal account of the vision, or to identify verbally the nature of the spirit power. It came to be known instead through observation of his behavior (Spier and Sapir, 1930:238).

Here, then, it is through attention to physical detail in body movement, or to communication visually received, that the interpretation of a person's behavior is primarily accomplished. This same emphasis on attention to physical detail is also strongly expressed in local Indian myths. In these myths, a trickster figure, or one who is attempting to deceive other actors in the myth, is often caught through his failure completely to conceal evidence that runs counter to the interpretation or framing of events he is attempting to perpetrate. Thus in one myth in which Coyote turns himself into a baby, so that he may receive the sympathy of women fishing along the river and be fed their fish, he is revealed by the women's spotting of the pubic hair that he neglected to eliminate in his self-transformation.[3] Thus, too, in "Skunk and Eagle" (Jacobs, 1929; but also told to me by a Warm Springs resident), Skunk conceals a woman who has come to marry Eagle, but the woman subtly reveals her own presence by repeatedly placing one of her long hairs in the bowl of roots to be eaten by Eagle, who, by attending to the anomaly of the hair, discovers Skunk's deception.

Hymes' discussion of Clackamas Chinook myths (Hymes, 1968) argues for attention to physical detail in the *auditory* as well as the visual channel. Thus, in his analysis of the Clackamas Chinook myth recorded by Jacobs, "Seal and Her Younger Brother Dwelt There," Seal's daughter hears a dripping sound several nights in a row that alarms her. While her mother encourages her to interpret this noise as routine and innocuous, the sound is later revealed as having been a forewarning of Seal's brother's death.

There are other cultural contexts where attention to auditory detail is stressed. In the vision quest, the spirit is identified by its characteristic animal cry, and its special spirit song, as well as its appearance. The spirit also verbally explains the specific power that is being conferred (Murdock, 1962:166). In the Winter Dances where the distinctive dance of a dancer may reveal his spirit, although not his particular gift of power, the song characteristic of that spirit is also sung (Murdock, 1962:167). In general, then, there is an assumption and encouragement of the ability to attend to and interpret behavioral subtlties in both the auditory and visual channels.

It should be evident, then, that Warm Springs culture in many ways reinforces a form of receptive competence in both the visual and auditory channels that facilitates awareness of the more subtle bids for attention made by Indian speakers. This suggests that Warm Springs Indians meet the condition that a hearer or hearers *receive* the speakers signaling for attention in a culturally distinctive manner.

Once a hearer is aware of a speaker's bid for attention, the hearer must behave in such a way as to *convey attention,* so that the speaker will know that the hearer is paying attention and the speaker can continue to speak. This third necessary condition for the successful transmission of the linguistic message is fulfilled through expression of the productive communicative competence of the listener. In other words the listener must behave so that the speaker can infer that attention is being paid. Again, Indian and Anglo ways of meeting that condition differ.

In some fundamental ways, Indian and Anglo uses of the visual channel to convey listening behavior are similar. Both Indian and Anglo listeners usually face the speaker. Warm Springs Indians do, however demonstrate a stronger preference for facing one another than Anglos do. That preference is most evident in large-scale general council meetings and social events where seating is usually around the edges of the room. When chairs are placed in rows at such gatherings as they are for Anglo audiences, people sometimes pull them back against the wall so that they reduce the number of people behind them and increase the number of people they are facing.

In both Anglo and Warm Springs Indian interaction, active physical involvements are abandoned when there is talk to attend to, as if to free the mind for the processing of information received auditorally rather than visually. But Indian listeners are stiller. They generally do not fidget and change postural position to the extent that anglo listeners do, as if they were capable of staying in place longer.

Both facing and stillness are, however, behaviors that can be directed to those present in a general manner. They convey interactional involvement in a shared focus of attention, rather than designating a particular person as speaker. There are other sorts of behavior that convey attention more directly to a particular person.

Nodding as the speaker speaks, particularly at junctures in the speech, conveys attention to the speaker in particular. And when a listener gazes in the speaker's face more often than in the faces of others, this too conveys greater attention to that particular person. Where two or more persons speak at once, listening behavior that designates a speaker can determine who will continue speaking, or who will get the floor.

Both nodding and gazing, as forms of designative behavior, are common in Anglo interaction. Such behavior not only designates the speaker, but also constitutes a way in which some hearers can select themselves as listeners. In other words, some of those who are conveying general attentiveness through alignment and lack of physical activity may nod and gaze at the speaker more than others. We would say that some pay more attention than others. People on the Warm Springs Reservation engage in less of this designative activity. They nod less and do not gaze so much more often at the speaker than at others, when compared with Anglos. This means that some do not select or designate themselves as listeners, or engage in listening behavior that differentiates some as being more attentive than others. The most directed and designative behavior that listeners engage in is change in facial expression in reaction to the speaker's words, particularly change in the area around the eyes.

It is important to mention here that Warm Springs listeners generally do not gaze into the faces of either the speaker or the other listeners to the extent that Anglos do. Thus the Indian speaker receives less visual feedback from listeners for two different reasons: First, like Indian speakers, Indian listeners do not look in the faces of cointeractants as much as Anglo listeners. Second, Indian listeners do not look in the faces of speakers more than hearers as much as Anglo listeners do.

In the *auditory* channel, the ways in which Warm Springs Indians convey attention run parallel to their use of the visual channel. Silence, or the absence of talk by listeners is for both Anglo and Indian listeners a way of conveying that they are attending to the talk of another. But in Anglo interaction that silence is often interspersed with brief comments, "yeses" and "mmm hmmms" from listeners at appropriate junctures. These interjections serve the same function as head nods in that they convey that the listener is attending. And just as Warm Springs Indians nod less than Anglos, so too they provide fewer verbal interjections as listeners that convey they are attending.

The second way in which the auditory channel can be used by listeners to convey attention to a speaker is through response to the speaker. Sacks (1967) has discussed the way in which an utterance can demonstrate having heard the last speaker. Thus, for example when one says "That's what I mean," the "that" usually refers to antecedent speech, although it can refer to nonverbal behavior as well. And such an utterance will be taken to show that the speaker heard the previous speaker who said whatever "that" refers to. The replacement of nouns with pronouns, as in

> A: I saw John yesterday.
> B: Oh, how is he?

is one of the most widespread devices for linking one utterance to another and demonstrating having heard at the same time. Another widespread linking device involves the deletion of verb phrases and the retention of the noun in subject position and the auxiliary verb, as in

> 1. A: He's a nice guy.
>   B: Yes he is.
>
> 2. A: Can she come with us?
>   B: Sure she can.

Question and answer sequences in particular draw very heavily on deletion of this sort in linking the response to the initiation.

In Warm Springs interaction, listeners provide less evidence of attention through the response to the speaker than in Anglo interaction. To begin with there are longer pauses between speakers' turns at talk. Thus, even though the average difference between Anglo and Indian length of pause between turns is quite small, it is still the case that the person who just spoke must wait longer before receiving a response that may or may not provide evidence in the auditory channel that the hearer is attending.

In addition, one's impression of Warm Springs interaction is that overall there is less of the sort of local management of topics or close interdependence between adjacent utterances that Sacks (1967) describes for Anglo conversation, and consequently less syntactic interdependence of adjacent turns at talk. This difference between Anglos and Indians is not equally in evidence in all Warm Springs interaction. It is more apparent in large-scale events involving a number of speakers over an extended period of time. The General Councils that are held about once a month on the reservation illustrate the more global management of topics.

General Councils are open to the entire reservation and are usually announced at least a week in advance on signs posted in places frequented by many tribal members. Such meetings often begin with the presentation of information by one or several persons. These persons may be council members or tribal administration personnel reporting on tribal business. Sometimes they are outsiders, such as tribally hired architects or lawyers, or school personnel, providing information about their work that is relevant to tribal members.

Later the floor is opened to tribal members who then make comments and ask questions. Sometimes the subjects raised during this second phase of the meeting will have nothing to do with topics on which information was earlier provided. And some meetings are almost entirely given over to the period when the floor is open to all.

At one such General Council meeting, where the topic announced on signs for the meetings was "Forest Product Industries," a report on the earnings and prospective earnings of the saw mill was given by the men who manage the mill. After several questions about the timber industries an old woman spoke in English. She said that (1) tribal members never get anything back from their investments; (2) a certain person (whom she named) took a trip to Washington, D.C.; (3) the interpreter doesn't interpret her correctly (when she speaks in Sahaptin and her talk is interpreted in English);

(4) certain persons (whom she named) go to Washington to make laws. And she concluded with the question: "Why can't the people sell fish from Sherar's Bridge?" There was then a one-second pause. Then a man spoke saying "I don't have any questions, but I heard a statement I want to speak on. Someone said we have to move ahead." Then he went on to make a general statement supporting the mill operation and urging that more young men from the tribe seek jobs there.

Fifteen minutes later, after eight other persons had spoken, in the context of discussion of a report given during that fifteen minutes from a member of the Fish and Wildlife Committee on the laws regulating commercial fishing, the first person named by the first speaker said: "I've taken a lot of trips to Washington and I can account for every one of them."

Half an hour later, after further discussion of both timber and fishing, a woman spoke. She asked whether tags are supposed to be attached to the fish nets, a question that was answered. Then she said that the older people think they are supposed to get first access to fish caught on a certain day and to be given the fish, and she didn't know where they got that idea. She said, "I would like to be related to all of them, would like to be related to—(the first speaker who had posed a question 45 minutes earlier), but we have to think of our own family first."

In this way, two and possibly three of the first woman's concerns were responded to: the first man's generally supportive statement can be interpreted as a response to the old woman's claim that tribal members do not get anything back on their investments. The trips to Washington and the fishing problems were also eventually dealt with much later, as I have noted, however obscure the responses may seem to the reader. The criticism of the interpreter (who was present) was never taken up.

Note then that (1) in all of this, neither the first woman nor those who responded to her ever spoke directly to one another, although they did refer to one another by name; (2) the first woman never called for a response to her statements; and (3) the "responses" that were forthcoming were widely separated from speech to which they were a response, and no effort was made to connect them to one another beyond what I have reported here. It may be worth noting that with this approach to sequencing, conflict between persons can be muted and obscured.

In everyday conversations the lesser extent of local management of topics is most apparent in Warm Springs Indians' responses to questions. While some questions are answered immediately, not all are. There does not seem to be the obligation that Anglos abide by to give *some* kind of response. Questions are often answered some time after they have been asked. There is accordingly less syntactic linking between a question and the utterance of the next speaker overall.

Both the infrequency of verbal back channel work and the lesser amount of syntactic linking by the next speaker to the last speaker's utterance result in less designation of the speaker as well.

The *speaker's recognition of the hearer's behavior as conveying attention* is the fourth condition that must be met for the successful transmission of a linguistic message. The speaker must realize that attention is being paid. Otherwise the speaker will not continue to speak, and will not perceive that the message has been successfully transmitted.

The differences between Anglo and Indian ways of conveying attention to the speaker have implications for the way in which Indian speakers determine whether they are in fact being attended to. From the Anglo point of view, Indian listeners use fewer sources of information to provide evidence of attention to the speaker. There is less back channel work in both the visual and auditory channels in the Indian interaction. In addition, in both channels, attention is conveyed in a general manner, rather than being designative, or directed by only certain listeners toward a specific speaker. Thus in the visual channel, it is the fact that Indian listeners face their cointeractants, including the speaker, and are still that the speaker must rely on. And in the auditory channel, it is the silence of those the Indian speaker addresses that provides the evidence of attention.

There is some evidence that the gaze direction of the Indian listener in particular is interpreted in a qualitatively different way than in Anglo interaction. I have suggested that the area around the eyes is for Indian speakers and hearers a behaviorally expressive region. Speakers' talk is modified by widening and crinkling of the muscles around the eyes. Hearers' attention is to some degree conveyed by changes in facial expression that involve movement in the area around the eyes. Yet at the same time, hearers do not look into speakers' faces and speakers do not look into the listeners' faces as much as in Anglo interaction. This would suggest an odd pattern of information exchange in which the most expressive region of the face is the least attended to. There is, however, other evidence to suggest that both gaze direction and expressiveness are given a great deal of attention, and that the eyes are considered very powerful messages senders.

The eyes are, first of all, treated as central to Indian appearance, or as an aspect of appearance that is closely attended to by others and judged by aesthetic standards. Mel Jacobs notes the general importance of eyes in his analyses of Clackamas Chinook myths. In explicating Wren's treatment of several other myth personalities in "Wren and His Father's Mother," Jacobs notes:

> In each instance he ridicules their eyes, very likely in a context like that of other myths where a person's eyes, which are important in one's self-identity, are referred to depreciatingly and humorously because they are structurally aberrant. (Jacobs, 1958:141)

On the Warm Springs Reservation, tribal members similarly were notably concerned with the appearance of their eyes, and noted peculiarities in the shape and coloring of their own eyes and of others that were not readily observable to me. Persons with temporary eye damage caused by infections or bruising were reluctant to appear in public, and would not do so without concealing their eyes, usually with sunglasses. In Indian social activities calling for the use of ritual paraphernalia, particularly in war dancing, decoration and paint were used to draw attention to and enhance the eyes to a much greater degree than other parts of the face or body.

Similarly, in providing accounts of people's reactions and responses to ongoing events, the information gleaned from the eyes is treated as definitive and as indicative of true feelings, so that one hears accounts such as, "And when he heard that, his eyes opened real wide," and, "He just looked at her," and, "They were snapping eyes;" each typically accompanied by a demonstration of the eye movements described by the teller. Such accounts occur much more often in Indian characterizations than they do in non-Indian characterizations of this sort.

Concealment of the eyes is in certain circumstances almost ritualized, and such concealment is explicitly explained as due to the concern not to reveal what one is thinking. This is particularly true of eye concealment that occurs in Indian gambling, where the game proceeds through one side's guessing in which hand one of two bones is held by a person on the other side. In this play, the persons holding and hiding the bones typically cast their eyes down, with the explicit account of this being that they do not want the guesser on the other side to read their minds.

From this it should be apparent that there is also a sense in which the eyes are seen as capable in themselves of sending strong messages. This idea is most explicit and intense in the belief that it is possible if one has spirit power to curse a person, intentionally or unintentionally, through looks, and more specifically, through looking at a person when one is angry or jealous. This belief is sometimes cited as a reason for covering babies when they are taken out in public. And people who are acting in such a way as to draw attention to themselves are sometimes warned of their vulnerability to such cursing.

Persons with great spirit power, including Indian doctors or "shamans", are those most likely to be seen as having done such cursing. Today, deaths and serious illnesses are often given more than one explanation. A medical account will be given, but at the same time, the death will be reconstructed as having been caused by a particular encounter between the deceased and a person with spirit power who, on some public occasion, expressed anger toward the deceased and glared at him. People are apparently thought to be particularly vulnerable to such acts when their backs are turned.

Persons who have survived such curses, due to supernatural protection of their own, will recall having experienced the feeling of being hit in the back of the head when they turned away from someone who was angry. People may be warned not to turn their back on and to stay away from persons known to be jealous of them or angry at them. That concern may account for the discomfort older people are said to feel at General Council meetings (events that such acts are not uncommonly traced back to) when the traditional seating arrangement for the audience is replaced with the non-Indian arrangement of rows of persons all facing the same direction.

One finds evidence of a similar sort in the *Wishram Ethnography* of Spier and Sapir:

> When a shaman visits at their home the children must remain very quiet. In particular they must not run behind his back. To pass behind his back when he does not see it may frighten him, disturb his spirit, and cause him harm. They must also be careful not to drop anything, to make a sudden report, so that he is startled. If they do, he gets angry and may bewitch some member of the family. (Spier and Sapir, 1930:248)

The power of the eyes is perhaps most dramatically expressed in the myths that provide accounts of the doings of powerful gamblers. In such accounts, the powerful one usually keeps his head down or covered, unless approached directly by another or antagonized, and then, by merely glancing up, he burns the person. For example:

They (two sat down) and then they (all the men) gambled. They (the two boys) defeated him completely. Now he (the headman) said, "When now did your village turn?" Whereupon something (Crawfish) came out from a bed, he went, he took discs. They (two) watched him, he began to cheat at the discs. He (the younger brother) looked at him (at Crawfish), *his eyes became red* (from the flame), *they popped out* [italics mine]. He went groping away. They (the people) said 'Holy mackeral!'. Now our chief has encountered something (that can match his spirit-power)! (Jacobs, 1958:128)

In this way, the peculiar marking of a variety of animals was accounted for.

Thus the eyes are assigned importance as sources of information in interaction, and within a symbolic framework, the eyes are represented as capable of sending very powerful messages indeed. An Indian speaker is likely to pay a good deal of attention to listeners' eyes, to determine how they are responding to his or her speech, even though the speaker may not look often or at length into the eyes of a given individual.

From this comparison of the visual and auditory means used by Anglos and Warm Springs Indians to convey attention and determine who others are paying attention to, it should be evident that the people of Warm Springs structure attention in a culturally distinctive manner. People of any culture are biologically equipped to send and receive information in both the visual and auditory channels in interaction structured through talk. For this reason, we find that both Anglos and Indians use the auditory and visual channel in basically the same manner. Thus they are always within a certain range when speaking, tend to face one another, and to rely on the same signaling sources in meeting the same conditions for the successful transmission of a linguistic message.

At the same time, Indian and Anglo interactants differ in the types and forms of signaling they rely upon most in each channel, in both productive and receptive communicative competence.

Regulation of Speaker Change

Earlier in this chapter, I suggested that each time there is a change of speakers the structure of attention is renegotiated in terms of who pays attention to whom. In this section I will consider how the differences between Anglo and Warm Springs Indian attention structures affect that renegotiation process through which speaker change is regulated.

In general Indian change of speakers involves less control over the turns of others and more control over one's own turn. There are basically two differences between Anglo and Indian attention structures which contribute to the contrast in patterns of control. The first is the lesser frequency of designative activity in Indian interaction. The second relevant difference is the relative freedom from topical and syntactic constraints placed on the next speaker by the current speaker in Indian interaction.

When Anglo speakers designate listeners (by conveying that their speech is directed to some more than others), this increases the likelihood that the persons so designated will be the next speaker. There are good reasons why the person most directly addressed is more likely than others to be the next speaker. By directing talk to particular individuals, the speaker conveys more interest in their responses than in the responses of others. The listener being addressed can thus be sure that at least the person addressing the listener will attend if that listener becomes the next speaker. In addition, if the current speaker has spoken in such a way that only some present can understand what is being said, those who understand may be the only people present in a position to respond in a meaningful way.

The common Anglo expectation that the next speaker's turn at talk will be topically and syntactically related to the current speaker's utterance also sets up constraints that must be met by the next speaker. Thus the current speaker in Anglo interaction can influence both who speaks next and what is said by the next speaker. In Warm Springs Indian interaction, the relative infrequency of speaker designation of listeners and the looser constraints on topic and syntactic relatedness between adjacent speakers' utterances allows for the individual interactant to have more control over when to speak and what to say. This control is most evident in handling responses to questions.

The Indian control over own turns at talk is facilitated by other features of speaker change regulation besides those related to the attention structure. There is almost no interruption of one speaker by another in Warm Springs talk. Thus speakers control not only when they will speak, and what they will speak about, but also how long they will speak and when they will finish speaking. What's more, talk among Warm Springs Indians is more evenly distributed than it is among Anglos: there is less variation in length of turns, and it is less often the case that some people will have many more turns at talk than others during the course of a conversation. In other words, people rarely abuse or take advantage of the self-control they are allowed to exercise to dominate a conversation; they avoid talking more than others in a way that would draw attention to themselves.

Given a system for the regulation of talk in which speakers usually determine when they will talk, one might expect a higher occurrence of more than one person beginning to speak at the same time. However, this is not the case. Rarely do two people begin to talk at the same time. The pause between the talk of two different speakers is typically longer than in Anglo conversation. This allows people to be sure that the last speaker has finished speaking. It also allows people to plan their utterances in advance. It may also allow people time to seek visual evidence that others are not themselves preparing to speak, but ultimately the absence of multiple initiations of talk remains something of a mystery.

In large-scale events involving the regulation of speaker change among many persons, there is again a contrast between Anglo and Indian ways of institutionalizing the allocation of turns. In the Anglo settings for large-scale events, like churches, courtrooms, and class-rooms, it is common to have one position and one person in that position who directs the interaction. Thus persons in such a position, like judges and teachers, determined who will speak when and for what purpose. In a variety of social settings, Anglos delegate someone as "chairman" of the meeting.

In large-scale Indian events, there is less often a single position in the interactional structure from which such directing is done. More often there will be several persons involved in directing others, or the regulation of interaction will be predetermined by some ritual principle. For example, in traditional religious activities, where worship dancing goes on, the drummer-singers take turn leading songs, and they share the responsibility for getting the dancers started dancing with the ritual leader who rings a bell at a certain juncture in the singing. The movement pattern of food servers at the Root and Huckleberry Feasts at the long house is determined by religious custom, not verbal directions. When a position does entail overseeing the activity of others, such a position usually can be and is occupied serially by more than one person. For example, even though the tribal chairman is the official expected to preside over General Councils he usually turns over the meeting completely to other people who introduce topics and speakers.[4]

Warm Springs noncontrolling regulation of interaction both reflects and expresses the value that Warm Springs Indians explicitly hold, of not putting oneself above others. That value is expressed through efforts to avoid exerting control over others and to avoid directing attention to one's self or others.

From the characterization of Warm Springs use of the auditory and visual channels provided in this chapter, it should be apparent that both receptive and productive communicative competence in structuring attention are culturally different from Anglo communicative competence.

We may view the behavior that has been discussed as constituting the adult model for the children of Warm Springs during the first six years of their lives.

Notes

1. As the tribal bureaucracy expands, and Indians gradually replace non-Indians in administrative positions, the number of white-collar jobs for Indians is increasing.
2. The Shaker Church is an Indian Christian church.
3. The version of this myth used here was told to me by a Warm Springs resident.
4. See Philips (1975b) for a more detailed discussion of Warm Springs regulation of interaction.

5

Visual and Auditory Socialization

In this chapter we will consider the ways in which the socialization of Warm Springs children shapes their use of the visual and auditory channels of communication.

Chapter 3 discussed the continued social segregation of the Indians of Warm Springs to explain how and why Indian children engage in interaction primarily with other Indians, until they start school. Chapter 4 described the adult communicative behavior that constitutes the children's model of behavior. In this chapter, attention will focus on the ways in which the socialization of children contributes to the acquisition of the same sort of communicative competence their parents display.

The Learning Environment

All societies have theories of how learning takes place, even if those theories must be inferred from behavior rather than expressed in metacommunicative activity. At Warm Springs one has the sense that both consciously and unconsciously *visual reception* is given priority as a general mode of learning. In addition, productive competence in the form of physical activity conveyed in the visual channel is the primary way in which Indian children demonstrate both comprehension of what they have received and the mastery of new skills.

That emphasis on visual learning is consistent with the general allocation in public life of physical skills to the younger and verbal skills to the older that was discussed in Chapter 4. The emphasis on visual learning is also consistent with the focus on the power of the eyes in symbolic activities.

A general emphasis on reception in both the visual and auditory channels is evident in the treatment of children. Warm Springs infants, like children and adults, spend more of their time in the presence of other people than is true of Anglo middle-class babies. Even when asleep during the day they spend much less time in rooms alone. And because it is unusual for older people to be alone, the supervision of children can be shared.

Most babies are put on cradleboards for short periods soon after birth. The board can be laid on a piece of furniture or propped up against a wall. Indian infants on cradleboards are taken out in public at earlier ages (within two weeks of birth) and for longer periods than Anglo babies.

There is some evidence that older kinsmen assume a priority of the visual channel over the auditory in the infants' processing of information. As indicated above, babies on cradleboards are propped up vertically so that they can see what is going on. To facilitate sleep, the board is laid flat and often covered even when the baby is wide awake. In this way, visual stimulation is completely cut off, while auditory stimulation is not, suggesting an orientation to the visual as the channel more compelling of attention. With Anglo middle-class infants, by contrast, greater efforts are made to cut off auditory stimulation to provide a soothing environment.

Older Indian children engage in a great deal of intentional learning through watching others. They will stand by the side of older adults while the latter cook, sew, or chop wood. While they are not frequently exhorted to do this, old women recall being urged by their elders to watch adult activities so they would learn. There is considerably less in the way of the verbal explanation of how to do something before it is attempted than is so common in Anglo middle-class families. And young children are encouraged to demonstrate their understanding of the information they have received through physical action conveyed in the visual channel.

That emphasis on the expression of physical competence is evident in the way children acquire langauge. The auditory channel is not ignored or neglected in the socialization of the child, but it is used in a qualitatively different way. Older kinsmen talk to infants a good deal, although probably not as much as Anglo middle-class caretakers. They less often make efforts to elicit sounds, or words, from the babies, and make fewer attempts to incorporate the sounds the babies do make into the interaction. In other words, Indian adults less often interpret babies' vocalizations, or respond to them as if something meaningful has been said.

In keeping with the infrequency of efforts to elicit and interpret sounds, there is more emphasis given to the child's receptive linguistic competence than to productive competence as he reaches first the one-word and then the two-word stages of utterance construction. Thus children are given many directions and then watched closely to see if they do what they are told. If they do what they are told, it is taken as evidence of comprehension.

The pattern of interaction just described may result in the Indian child being exposed to different frequencies of particular syntactic forms than Anglo children. For example, Indian children may hear imperative forms (e.g., "Go get it," "Bring it here," "Give Mary some.") relatively more often and question forms relatively less often.

In part such a pattern of socialization is possible because of an emphasis on the encouragement of early physical self-sufficiency, so that one-year-old Indian children will be more often told to get food for themselves from the kitchen, or to bring their caretakers clothing they are to be dressed in.

In the socialization for physical competence, the child's management of his own body is initially developed through tactile communication with older kinsmen. Physical contact between Indian infants and their caretakers is much more constant than in Anglo middle-class families.[1] The babies are held more of the time, and they are passed from one kinsman to another. Through such contact attention is given to developing the baby's body control. Infants no more than two months old are balanced on the palm of an adult's hand. Soon after that they are rapidly brought up over the adult's head and down again, and tossed in the air. During such play, one can see the baby visibly struggling to maintain balance and control. Before a child reaches the age of six months, adults will engage in playful wrestling and boxing with him rolling around on the floor while carefully protecting his body, and interpreting his random arm movements as punches to be responded to in kind.

At the same time, there is a concern to maintain a state of non-excitation or calmness in the baby.[2] Few attempts are made to elicit behavioral evidence of excitation. Babies are not tickled to make them gurgle, squeal, and flail about. When older children engage in play with babies likely to produce such excitation (e.g., spinning them about to make them dizzy), they are told to stop by their elders. Babies balanced and tossed by adults typically neither squeal nor give evidence of panic through spasmodic movement. Anglo visitors to the reservation sometimes comment on the relative infrequency of vocalization in such activity.

Related to this maintenance of calmness in the child is the absence of a special affection mode in tactile contact. Even after the child has been walking for some time, he continues to be held a great deal by his relatives, and to seek other forms of contact by sitting quite close to or learning against others. Squeezing, hugging, and kissing are used to convey affection among Anglos, and seem designed to produce an intensification of positive emotional affect. Those expressions are rarely observed between Indian children and their elders, let alone between Indian adults. Between adults the hand shake, a mere touching without squeeze, is the only common form of bodily contact other than that arising from people sitting close to one another. Thus while contact in which the child melds his body against that of another in relaxed stillness is common, contact that intensifies emotion is relatively lacking. And by the time children are two, they are expected and are able to sit quite still for several hours at a time at public gatherings and during adult conversation at home.

We see in this very early training the basis for the relative physical stillness of both speakers and hearers in adult Indian interaction discussed in Chapter 4.

Most families initiate more formal training in bodily control by the age of two. Specifically, both boys and girls begin to be taught how to fight, how to dance, and how to ride a horse. And before they reach school age, they are learning the skills of team sports from their older siblings and cousins. Of course not all families train their children in all of these skills, but there are few families in which instruction in at least one of these areas is not taking place by this age.

In sum, the socialization of children for interaction which is organized through physical activity communicated in the visual channel is given more attention, both in play and informal training, than socialization for communication in the auditory channel. There is dual emphasis on both control in action and control in inaction. The emphasis on physical control prepares them well for the special roles they assume in the public life of the community that were discussed in Chapter 4.

Social Control of Warm Springs Children

It is also possible to see the ways in which the social control of Indian children encourages an adult interactional system in which individuals control their own activity, but do not attempt to control the actions of others, as was described in Chapter 4.

First the socialization of children is lacking in authority concentration. Warm Springs Indian children are accustomed to being raised by a number of people. Their grandparents, uncles and aunts, older siblings, and cousins are among those who can come to play an active role in their socialization.

When a child is perceived to be acting alone and is thought to be behaving inappropriately, the child is taken aside and spoken to privately so that the attention of others present will not be drawn to that child in a way that could be humiliating.

But Warm Springs children are less often disciplined as individuals and more often disciplined as a group than is true of Anglo middle-class children. It is siblings and cousins, rather than neighbor children or the children of parents' friends, who play together at Warm Springs. Warm Springs children spend more time with their peers in relation to the amount of time spent with adults than is true of Anglo children. When they quarrel among themselves, or become noisy, careless, or destructive, the older person who intervenes does not seek to establish and assign individual blame and sanction. Rather, the group as a whole is held accountable. Older people reminisce about the days when there was a "whip man" who came around annually and whipped all of the children for the wrongdoings of any of them that had been reported to him by elder kinsmen.[3] By enforcing collective responsibility, children are provided with the foundations for sustained cooperative activity.

These are some of the aspects of Warm Springs interaction that lead one to characterize the culture as emphasizing cooperative activity and egalitarian relationships, and contributing to a system in which people exert little direct interactional control over one another.

There are other ways in which self-control is supported as well. At Warm Springs people may try to verbally convince others to take particular actions, try to "give them advice," or "make them listen," but they avoid punitive action if advice is not taken. People who are angry or sad and withdraw from social interaction are to be left alone until they come out of their nonsociable state voluntarily. There is a story, said to be well known on the reservation and considered humorous by some old people, that comes close to articulating this principle by demonstrating the consequences of adhering to it too strictly. In the story a man goes off by himself in anger. As night comes of his wife prepares the evening meal, lays it out, and calls to him to come and eat. He neither comes to the meal nor responds to her call. The next night she does the same thing, and again there is no response. The next night, the same thing again, and so on for five nights. Finally when there is no response on the fifth night, she goes to him, only to discover he is dead. While the humor of this story may be lost through its rendering here, its instruction in the consequences of carrying a good thing too far should be apparent.

This noncoercive cultural orientation, is evident also in day-to-day dealings that do not necessarily entail conflict of any sort between the parties involved. Most notable in adult interactions is the verbal formulation of requests and invitations in such a way that a commitment by the respondent to fulfill the request or respond to the invitation is not required. Thus a person will state a need (e.g., "Johnnie has to be taken to the hospital today" or, "I've got to get all of this food cooked."), rather than asking a question ("Will you take Johnny?" or, "Can you help me cook this food?"). Similarly, people inform others of gatherings to be held and events that will occur, rather than asking them if they want to come or will come. I was told when I first began to visit people on the reservation that if a meal was served while I was at someone's house, I should assume I was included among those who would eat, and not wait for an invitation to join in, or assume I should leave if not given an invitation. Anglos working on the reservation who have found it difficult to become involved in Indian social life have indicated they are rarely invited to Indian homes, but they have been told that they are welcome any time, just as they are welcome at longhouse affairs. While it may not be strictly true that one should always attend such affairs, visit homes, and sit down to eat without being invited, these instructions are intended to convey the ways in which the individual is expected to make the choice to come forward or not without having to make a commitment in advance.

In the socialization of children, there are several ways in which this "self-determination" (French 1955:160) is allowed and even encouraged. Children are expected to be self-sufficient at a relatively early age. When Indian adults were asked how they felt their ways of rearing children differed from those of Anglo parents, their responses often focused on allowing children to learn for themselves. Thus it was suggested that if an Indian child were warned not to touch a hot stove, and proceeded to do so anyway, he would not be prevented physically from doing so, but would be allowed to learn by experiencing the consequences, if no real harm would be done. An Anglo parent, it was argued, would be more likely to physically prevent the child from burning himself.

Warm Springs Indian children are encouraged to care for themselves at younger ages than Anglo children. They are also encouraged to help as soon as they are able to follow simple verbal directions, even if the help is no more than carrying an object from one part of the house to another. By the age of eight, many girls are expected to be able to carry out most of the domestic activity entailed in running a household. Boys of this age are expected to be able to care for the farm animals in the rural areas, and to handle a gun. By the age of ten, children in many families may be away from home for many hours without informing an older adult of their whereabouts. Children of that age are considered old enough to choose where they live. If a child does not come home at all at night, his home kinsmen are likely to assume he is staying at the home of another close relative. Quite frequently, those he has been living with will be informed by other relatives the next day that the child has decided to stay with them for awhile. While children change residence for a number of reasons, such a move is often the remedy for resolving or avoiding conflict between the child and his caretakers in the home from which he moves. Physical punishment of children is rare. It is not unusual to hear an exasperated caretaker say, "I talk to him and I talk to him, but he just won't listen." The implication here is that this is all one can do.

In general, then, the authority over Warm Spring children is distributed over a greater number of people. Both individual autonomy and collective group responsibility are fostered in a way that encourages control over oneself but not control over others.

It has been my purpose in this chapter to discuss the nature of the relationship between adult Indian communicative behavior and the ways in which Indian children are socialized. One point of that discussion is that when Indian children first start grade school at the age of six, they are already well on their way to being Indian adults. The children have already learned to communicate and to learn in culturally distinctive ways.

In the chapters to follow, we will consider what happens to the Indian children when they enter the school system, where the organization of interaction and the structuring of learning are derived from Anglo cultural traditions.

Notes

1. Montagu (1971) claims people in *most* societies provide their babies with more physical contact than is typical in mainstream American families.
2. Montagu (1971) argues that the contact through close swaddling of the type provided by cradleboards is conducive to calmness and security in infants.
3. French (1955) discusses the role of this "disciplinarian" in more detail.

Part III

Communication in the Classroom

Getting the Floor in the Classroom

Introduction

In traditional grade school classrooms, children are expected to master not only the content of curriculum material presented by the teacher, but also the socially appropriate use of communicative resources through which such mastery is demonstrated. In this chapter, I will describe some of the fundamental features of the organization of interaction in the classroom that children must learn if they are to communicate in a socially appropriate and meaningful fashion. The chapter that follows will then compare the participation of Warm Springs Indian and Anglo students in classroom interaction, drawing on the past chapters on Warm Springs to explain why their participation differs in ways that it does.

Classroom interaction does not always involve all those within classroom walls in a single focused encounter. Often students will be grouped into several focused interactions, and these may differ in terms of the ways in which attention is conveyed and turns at talk are regulated within them. The organization of these multiple encounters constitutes a higher level or order of the organization of interaction beyond that which pertains to the regulation of interaction in a single encounter. It entails the systematic choice of types of encounters that can be sustained at the same time, the sequential ordering of such multiple encounters through time, and standard procedures for organizing the transition from one arrangement of encounters to another. A child's knowledge of socially appropriate communicative behavior in the classroom, then, will entail knowledge not only of the attention structure and regulation of speaker shifts for a single encounter, but also of the synchronic and diachronic relationships between encounters.

In addition, there is not just one but two systems for organizing encounters and the talk that occurs within them in the classroom. There is first the "official" structure of interaction, constituted of the interaction between teacher and students through which curriculum content is transmitted. Interaction in this official structure is controlled by the teacher. She initiates, regulates, and terminates all of the encounters that occur within the official structure.

However, the children regularly engage in covert exchanges with one another that take their attention away from the official interaction controlled by the teacher. Such exchanges typically have little to do with curriculum content. They are initiated and maintained by the children, although often terminated by the teacher because they are inappropriate within the framework of official interaction. The ways in which these largely covert encounters are accomodated and built around official interaction is systematic. This secondary and dependent system of communication will be referred to as the "infrastructure" of classroom interaction.

Considerable attention has been given to the official structure of interaction in educational literature. Many reports convey the impression that it is the only system of organized behavior that exists in the classroom. Yet behavior with in one system has important consequences for behavior within the other. In the following discussion, each system for organizing interaction, and the relationship between the two, will be described.

The Official Structure of Classroom Interaction

While the way in which talk is regulated in the official structure varies from one type of encounter to another, as will be discussed in some detail further on, there is a standard normative system for regulating talk between teacher and students that requires description, before variations of this pattern can be understood.

The distinction between "teacher" and "student" itself entails systematic and complementary definitions of possible addressor-addressee relations. In the regulation of talk, all students have essentially one kind of relation with the teacher and another with their fellow students. Other possible bases for differentiation of speakers and hearers, such as sex, familial socioeconomic status and age, are not used in the institutionalized differentiation of participants. However, the way in which the student-teacher role differentiation is organized is similar to role differentiations based on differences in age, social class, and occupation in other contexts.

That there is typically one teacher and many students is not trivial, for in the regulation of official addressor-addressee relations in the classroom, it is usually *only* the teacher and not other students who can enter into such relations with the students. While students are at any given moment differentiated by whether they may, or must, be *audience* to the speakings of their fellow students, a student is usually not supposed to address a fellow student directly, and accordingly ought not attend a peer if the latter attempts to speak to him.

This means that at any time interaction is being sustained through talk, the teacher will sustain one end of the floor. The teacher will be either addressor or addressee. The teacher as addressor may designate all, some, or one student as the desired listeners. Those the teacher does not address are differentiated according to whether they are within the encounter as audience, or outside it and defined as persons who are not supposed to be listening. The student who speaks should designate the teacher as the person whom the student wishes to have pay attention if the talk is to be ratified.

Translated into sequential shiftings of who has the floor, this differentiation means that whenever a student has the floor, the teacher was either the last person to speak, or is the next person to speak, or both, for the student can only be either responding to the teacher or initiating talk addressed to the teacher who is the appropriate respondant.

This particular system for regulating talk is maintained in part through the ways in which attention is conveyed in the visual channel. Quite often, while the teacher faces the students and the students face the teacher, the students do not face one another, and are consequently not in a position to receive information from one another that is conveyed nonverbally by the signaling sources on the front of the body. Thus it is difficult for the students either to convey to their peers that they are attending, or to receive visual evidence of whether or not they are being attended to, unless they turn around in their chairs.

Even in interaction where the children face one another, the pattern of gaze direction indicates that the teacher is always the addressed recipient of student talk. When a student is speaking, the teacher gazes in the direction of that student's face much more often than elsewhere. When the teacher then assumes the position of speaker, her gaze may focus on a specific student (often the one who has just spoken) or move around the group of students while speaking, until designating the next student to speak. Then the teacher's gaze focuses on that student.

While the teacher is speaking, the students look at the teacher much more often than elsewhere. And when a student is speaking, the student designates the teacher as the addressed recipient of the speech by looking at the teacher far more often than at fellow students. Peers, in turn, do not gaze at the speaker's face nearly as often as the teacher does. They look more often at the teacher listening than they look at the student who is speaking. As often as not, while one student is speaking, the other students do not look at anyone, but gaze off in the distance or downward.

This particular pattern of gaze direction supports an impression conveyed by the system for regulating talk that students are not supposed to play a role in regulating the talk of their peers. A child's claim to the floor is validated by the teacher, both verbally and visually, or not at all, in the official structure of talk.

Because there is only one teacher and there are many students, this arrangement essentially gives the teacher control over who has the floor. As both an addressor and an addressee, the teacher is essentially without competition. When a student speaks, that student cannot be said to have the floor unless the teacher attends. The teacher can choose to attend to another, or to speak. In either way, the teacher can effectively take the floor away from the student. While the student cannot choose among adressees, or having failed to gain the attention of one, find another; the teacher, at least theoretically, has no competitors for the attention of the students, and hence can choose among them. Thus, the teacher determines who is to be defined as speaker and through responding, the teacher determines who will be defind as having spoken.

In addition, the teacher controls or defines the juncture or point at which a shift in addressor-addressee relations occurs. The teacher may cut off a student's unfinished utterance by beginning to speak or by attending to another student because of the teacher's floor control. Students may not do this.

That the teacher may do this, and be deemed appropriate and acceptable in so doing, does not necessarily follow from the teacher's floor-sustaining position. Classroom interaction could hypothetically be regulated in such a way that while the teacher determined who spoke next, the student could still determine how long to speak, and be allowed to signal the juncture at which the student was giving up the floor. This is, in fact, often what occurs. For example, when the teacher calls on a student who has raised a hand, the teacher is implicitly conveying a promise to attend to the entire speaking of that child. However, it is nevertheless within the bounds of what is seen as appropriate to the position as "teacher" to interrupt in a way that would be seen as inappropriate if students did it.

The basic differentiation between teacher and student in addressor-addressee relations holds constant in all official classroom interaction, as does the attendant basis for determining who speaks to whom, and in what order, and for determining at what junctures the shifts in addressor-addressee relations that constitute sequencing will occur.

Allocating Student Turns at Talk

But while the teacher is always on one end of the floor, various students will hold the other end. One or a combination of several principles for allocating student turns at talk is used in determining which students will hold the speaking end of the floor and in what order they will hold it.

All of the principles used by the teacher in determining which student will talk next entail a concern with equalizing student's opportunities to have a turn at talk. This concern with allowing all students opportunity to talk is similar to the American commitment to equal educational opportunity. Just as it does not follow from a system of equal opportunity in education that all students will actually obtain equal educations, so too it does not follow that the equal opportunity to talk in class results in all students talking roughly the same amount.

There are three ways in which the equal opportunity to speak is provided by the teacher. The *first* is the request for a 'choral' response. Here the teacher speaks in a way that calls for a response, without indicating the means through which a respondant is to be designated. Without such indication, the typical reaction of the students is to call out answers together.

The *second* way in which teachers attempt to equalize the opportunity for all to speak is through the use of the "round." In a round, the teacher systematically calls on every student who is party to the interaction, one after another. Often they use a principle for ordering such turns that is considered arbitrary within mainstream culture. The teacher may order student turns by the alphabetical listing of their names, by going around a circle, up and down rows of desks, or alternating between boys and girls. When such a system is used, the students do not have the choice of responding; they are designated to speak by the teacher whether they want to or not.

In the *third* and most common format for ordering student turns, the teacher uses what can best by characterized as a modified "first-come, first-served" system. In this familiar system, the first child to raise a hand, or one of those among the first, is called on. Once a child has had a turn in this way that child cannot have another until all of the other students who want to have had the opportunity to speak. The length and type of segment of interaction during which only one turn per student is allowed varies considerably. The restriction can hold for a single question. Thus, a teacher may ask the same question over and over until getting an answer the teacher considers appropriate. During this time, those who have tried to answer the question will not be called on again until no children who have not already tried are raising their hands. Then as soon as an appropriate answer has been provided, the floor is again open to whoever raises his hand first. But this restriction of not talking again if one has already had a turn can also apply to larger interactional units, up to and including an entire encounter from beginning to end.

While these three formats for equalizing student access to turns at talk are often used separately, they are sometimes combined. The most typical system for regulating student turns is one in which the teacher tries to give everyone a turn sometime during the course of a single encounter or bounded interaction. Thus, in the early phases of a lesson, the teacher will can on those who raise their hands first, but as time goes on will ignore those who raise their hands first to call on a child who is raising a hand for the first time. Eventually, the teacher may even ignore the raised hands to call on a child who has not raised a hand if that child has not talked yet.

Because the teacher does not necessarily involve all of the students in a single interaction at one time, talk is organized to equalize not only student turns at talk within one single sustained encounter, but also student participation in the range of encounters that the teacher controls. There are four basic *types of encounters* that differ from one another primarily in the number of students involved in interaction with the teacher, but also in the nonverbal structuring of attention and in the principles used in regulating student turns at talk. The teacher may engage in interaction with the *whole class*, with a *small group*, or on a *one-to-one* basis with a single student. Thus, a student may be involved in an encounter comprised of the teacher and one, some, or all of the students. However, a student may also not be involved in interaction with the teacher at all, but instead be directed to focus attention on *desk work*. Desk work usually means reading or doing written assignments. Thus, the child engages in one-way nonverbal communication involving the visual reception of written messages.

These four ways of allocating student involvement, which will be referred to as "participant structures," are combined both synchronically and diachronically to produce a level of interactional organization within which the structuring of any single encounter is accomplished. In the discussion to follow, each of these four participant structures, and the system for organizing interaction that emerges through combining them, will be considered.

The first participant structure involves the whole class in interaction with the teacher. In other words, when it occurs, there are no other encounters being sustained within the classroom. Typically the teacher either uses the 'first-come, first-served principle in allocating students turns at talk, or elicits a choral response to her own talk.

There is a variant of this first participant structure that appears in the lower grades in the form of "Show and Tell," and in later grades in the form of individual reports. In this variant, the child assumes the teacher's interactional position under the teacher's guidance. The child in the teacher's position faces the students and they face the child while the teacher sits off to one side. The child who assumes the teacher's position looks at the other students while addressing them in a monologue. In this way, the child is given practice in the communicative behavior associated with the teacher's position. The students' lack of familiarity with the commanding role is evident in the tendency of the child put in this position to continue to try to designate the teacher as the addressed recipient of speech by facing and looking at the teacher, and ignoring the students. Often even up to the sixth-grade level, teachers feel compelled to instruct the students, "Talk to them, don't talk to me." Nor does the child *fully* assume the teacher's interactional perrogatives under such circumstances. When the student has finished a monologue and the floor is open to the other students to ask questions, it is the teacher who typically designates who will speak, and more often than not, the students will address their questions to the teacher rather than to the student who has just finished speaking.

This variant of the basic format for involving the whole class in a single encounter is not used often in classrooms. In the lower grades it is usually used for transmission of information considered tangential to curriculum content, and participation is voluntary, as in Show and Tell. In the higher grades, where the child is put in the teacher's position to give individual oral reports, occupation of the teacher's position is obligatory, and usually arranged by use of the round as a turn organizer. This variant is also sometimes used in the higher grades for class business conducted by an elected class president to plan a class trip or money-making project. It is in such discussions that a student is likely to most fully assume the interactional per-rogatives of the teacher, just as the other students are most likely to attend in the same manner that they typically attend to the teacher.

The second type of participant structure used in organizing interaction is the small group. Here the teacher engages in focused interaction with a portion of the class, usually five to ten students. In this small group, the teacher uses rounds of turns more often than other principles for allocating student talk, and the round is used more in this participant structure than in any other.

In order to make it possible for all students to have access to such small groups, they must either be duplicated in space, so that more than one small group interaction occurs at the same time, or duplicated through time, so that one small group after another is organized in interaction. When teachers have teacher-aides, more than one small group at a time can be ongoing, with the teacher's aide assuming the interactional position of the teacher. Yet whether or not this is the case, there will usually be some students who are not engaged in focused interaction with a teacher or a teacher substi-tute. At such times, the teacher directs them to allocate their atten-tion to individual desk work.

There is a variant of the small group, often referred to by teachers as the "group project" that provides students with the opportunity to assume some of the teacher's usual perrogatives in regulating student turns at talk, just as the Show and Tell variant does. In this arrangement, students are assigned to groups and directed to carry out some project collectively, like making a mural or conducting an experiment with electricity. In this context it is understood that the students will regulate their own interaction in accomplishing this end. The teacher often dictates to such groups what system they should use for regulating their interaction among themselves. More often then not, the teacher either appoints a lead-er for each group, or tells the students to select such leaders, who then are expected to regulate the interaction of their peers, much in the way that the teacher normally does.

As a rule, all of the students in the class are organized into several groups at the same time, rather than sequentially through time. Occasionally some students may be involved in a group pro-ject while others engage in small-group work with the teacher or focus their attention on individual desk work.

A third participant structure is that of the one-to-one involvement between the teacher and a single student. Such one-to-one encounters involve the teacher's allocation of turns at encounters with her, rather than turns at talk, and such turns are usually allocated on a first-come, first-served basis. These encounters usually occur during periods when all of the children are focusing their attention on desk work. A student with questions about such work either raises a hand, or approaches the teacher at the teacher's desk. The teacher follows the first-come, first-served principle more strictly in this situation than in any other.

The fourth participant structure, desk work, is one in which the child's attention is focused on written materials on the child's desk. Desk work cannot be considered a participant structure in the sense that others are. Here there is no interaction in which to participate. Communication in the auditory channel is precluded because it is assumed that the child cannot receive or produce the written messages involved in reading and writting if engaged in talk with another person. It is also assumed that the signaling source in this case (e.g., a book) is not capable of *receiving* messages of any sort.

Each of the four participant structures has particular advantages and disadvantages in providing students with access to curriculum content. And those advantages and disadvantages limit the extent to which any single arrangement comes to be dominant or used to the exclusion of the others.

Perhaps the chief advantage of engaging the whole class in interaction is that the information transmitted by the teacher to the students through this process need only be transmitted once. However, the teacher does not receive as much information from any individual student as is possible in the other arrangements. Moreover, students' attention seems to wander more to the degree that each student has less opportunity to address the teacher frequently and at length. If they are required to spend a great proportion of time listening to the teacher and to their peers, their attention wanders. The students *pay more attention* when each has more opportunity to talk. In addition, with the whole class, the teacher usually aims to sustain talk that is relevant and meaningful for all of the students. In practice, this results in dialogue that is boringly repetitious of things already known to some students and incomprehensible to others. In other words, the teacher working with the whole class is not in a good position to adapt the talk to the skill level best suited to the individual student.

In small-group interaction, each student is given the opportunity to talk a greater amount of the time. While this increases the students' attention, the repetitiveness of much of the exchange in small groups, particularly when one student after another is asked to read aloud from a text that all are following with their eyes, decreases their attention. Such groups can be and often are organized according to skill levels, so that for example, the best, average, and poor readers would be segregated into three separate groups. Many educators think that this works to the advantage of the most advanced group, and to the disadvantage of the lower groups. But for all students, interaction in such an arrangement has the potential to provide the teacher with a clearer picture of the quality of each student's comprehension of curriculum content. However, the process of providing the entire class with exposure to whatever is communicated in the small group is far more time consuming than involving the whole class in a single, sustained interaction to convey the same information.

The advantages and disadvantages of the one-to-one encounter between teacher and student are those of the small group intensified. The student has the opportunity to initiate such involvements and has even more opportunity to talk a greater amount of the time spent in such an encounter than is true in the small group. The teacher's speech is adapted to the student's particular framework of relevance and can focus on the aspects of curriculum that the child finds most troublesome. At the same time, much more time is required to provide all of the students access to such one-to-one encounters between teacher and student than is true of the other participant structures.

Desk work, the fourth type of allocation of student attention, is in most ways quite different from the other participant structures. It entails the reception of information through a written code that is transmitted in the visual channel. The fundamental goal of schools is still to teach students both to send and receive written messages through "the Three R's," reading, writing and arithmetic, or in other words to teach them how to communicate *without* engaging in face-to-face interaction. Interaction itself is used to teach this skill, and to teach children how to translate back and forth between the interactive and the noninteractive. Written communication has the virtue of not requiring the immediate presence of the persons doing the communicating, yet it is limited by that same feature because written communication does not allow for the adjustments and clarifications possible in face-to-face interaction.[1]

The rotation of delivery of curriculum content through the four participant structures is common practice in classrooms, and teaching manuals often dictate that material be handled in this way.

Thus, students may be assigned to read a particular story, then to discuss it with the whole class, then to go over new vocabulary items, or to read the same material aloud in a small-group arrangement. Implicit in this practice is the assumption that each arrangement somehow reinforces the learning that occurs in the other arrangements, and at the same time, presents it from a different angle, or with a different emphasis, in this way maximizing exposure to the content.

Given these four possible participant structures for allocating students' attention, and the educational concern to equalize students' access to interaction with the teacher, the ways of combining them at any given point in time, are limited.

In practice, the most common arrangements for allocating students' attention at a given point in time are: (1) interaction between the teacher and the whole class; (2) interaction between the teacher and one small group, while other students' attention is focused on desk work; and (3) interaction between the teacher and a single student while other students engage in desk work.

At some point in time any one of these three general arrangements comes to an end, and another arrangement begins through the teacher's direction. The possible sequential orderings of such arrangements are limited. Such a shift or rearranging may involve a change from one of the three general arrangements just described to another. Or, it may involve the repetition of the same general arrangement, but with a reallocation of the various students' involvement and attention. The teacher may, for example, repeat an arrangement where some students are involved in small-group work, while others focus on desk work, but the teacher will assign those who have been in the small group to do desk work, and assign some of those who have been doing desk work to become involved in a new small group.

There are differences in the ways the four participant structures are used at the different grade levels that reflect assumptions about the types of interactional arrangements children are capable of mananging successfully at different ages. At the first-grade level, all of the participant structures and combinations of them are used for shorter periods of time than at the sixth-grade level. In one day, a first-grade class typically goes through 10 to 20 changes in the interactional arrangement so that students rarely spend more than 15 minutes at a time in a single, sustained encounter. At the sixth-grade level, the classes average 5 to 10 changes in the interactional arrangement each day. This difference does not emerge from decisions made by individual teachers. It is deliberately built into the lesson plan alternatives available to teachers in their teaching manuals, and is based on the assumption that the attention span of younger children is considerably shorter than that of older children, and that they will stop paying attention to the material being taught if the interaction is sustained beyond 15 minutes.

The frequency with which particular participant structures are used also varies with grade level. In the lower grades, the students spend a greater proportion of their time engaged in verbal interaction with the teacher. The amount of time that sixth graders spend with their attention focused on desk work is much greater than it is at the first-grade level. As students' skill in written communication increases, and less verbal interaction is required for transmission of this skill, more time is spent acquiring information through written communication.

Of the time that teachers spend engaged in face-to-face interaction with students, more is allocated at the first-grade level to small-group interaction.[2] At the sixth-grade level, a greater proportion of interaction takes place in discussions involving the whole class than in small groups.

There are other age-related differences as well. In the lower grades, the participant structure variants in which the children are directed to assume some of the regulatory functions of the teacher (e.g., Show and Tell, and group-project formats) are used much less than at the sixth-grade level and/or used less for transmission of the core curriculum content that is measured by achievement tests. Thus, while Show and Tell commonly occurs at the first-grade level, it is used to allow children to talk about things that happen to them outside school, whereas in the sixth grade, it appears in the form of individual reports in which students communicate curriculum-related information to other students. Yet even in the sixth grade, the material communicated in this way is not material that the whole class will be held responsible for in a testing situation.

The group-project arrangement is not used at all in first grade. And while it is used at the sixth-grade level for scientific experiments and producing murals, plays, and class newspapers, such projects still do not deal with the aspects of curriculum content that children must acquire to be able to move onto the next grade.

This age-related selectivity in the use of interactional arrangements suggests that the younger children are *too* young to sustain interaction regulated by themselves in a manner that will allow them to learn the kinds of things schools are committed to teach. Indeed, in the first six grades, children are rarely provided with the opportunity to practice regulating interaction among themselves, let alone given practice in how to learn from one another in such a framework.

At any given point in time, it is usually possible to identify the particular general arrangement in use through the positioning, alignment, and gaze direction pattern of the students and teacher in the classroom; or in other words, to determine how involvement has been allocated. And changes in participants' positioning, alignment, and pattern of gaze direction mark the end of one general interactional arrangement and the beginning of another. At the same time, there are also interactional segments or units with beginnings and ends that are marked only by changes in the organization of verbal behavior. For example, the teacher may change the means she is using to allocate student turns at talk from a choral-response system to first-come, first-served system without this being marked by changes in the positioning and alignment of participants. She may also switch from one topic to another within a physical arrangement without its being visually evident.

In general, the overall pattern of the organization of participant structures and the allocation of students into those structures is constrained by the concern that all of the children in the classroom be given equal access to the interactional processes through which school curriculum is transmitted and that all of the students are given equal access to the floor.

Teacher Ratification and Incorporation of Student Talk

As the preceeding sections indicate, teachers do try to equalize student's access to the floor. But teachers also respond in different ways when students attempt to take the floor.

In Chapter 1, I discussed some of the many ways that speakers can determine whether they are being attended to, or listeners can convey that they are, in fact, paying attention. Anglos often use the *response* as a source of evidence of attention to speakers. They examine the response made to a speaker to determine whether that response shows evidence of the respondant's having heard the previous speaker.

In classroom interaction, the teacher's speech provides evidence of having heard the speech of *some* students, but not others. And in this way, some students' talk is ratified and incorporated in the sequence of discourse, while other students' speech is not. Not all ratification or failure to ratify is intentional. In general, however, that which is ratified or responded to has been judged by the teacher to be acceptable and appropriate. And generally that which is *not* ratified or responded to has either not been heard or understood by the teacher or has been judged inappropriate by the teacher.

There are several very common ways in which teachers ratify students' utterances, and incorporate features of those utterances into their own utterances. First, and most obviously, there is very direct ratification of student utterances, which occurs quite often when students are responding to questions the teacher has asked.

1. *Teacher*: They are ___. They're on what?[3]
   Student: On wheels.
   Teacher: Right you are, Barbara. They're on wheels.
   [7(2) WS1–626]

2. *Teacher*: Now *read* what he called down.
   Student: And up and up and up.
   Teacher: Right you are, Bobby, Did everyone find the word that says "Stop it."
   [6(1) WS1–57 (2)]

3. *Teacher*: Alright, Larry? Why would you rather sleep in a camper than a tent?
   Student: Cause if you sleep in a tent all the animals can set in.
   Teacher: Alright, Shane?
   [7(2) WS1–626]

Second, teachers use the same linking devices that pervade the use of English in discourse and give evidence that the speaker has heard what the last speaker said. They substitute pronouns for units of speech that appear in the student's utterances. For example, the teachers frequently use the demonstrative pronoun "that" to refer back to what a student has said:

4. *Teacher*: Mark started using his imagination and now he wants Daddy to use/Daddy's imagination/to tell some more/of the story/.
   Student: /On the moon?/ /on the moon?/
   Teacher: That's right. Daddy's gonna tell some more about Mark on the moon.
   [6(1) WS1–900]

5. *Student*: And then when she gets there, she's gonna stop it.
   Teacher: Yes. What does Dick think of that, Allen? Would you read what Dick said?
   [9(1) M 1/2–828]

Teachers also commonly substitute pronouns for nouns in the student's speech.

6. *Student:*   We always sleep in a *camper* that has a white thing,
                  cause it hases beds.
   Teacher: Do you sleep in *it* every night?
   [7(2) WS1–626]

7. *Teacher:*   Who do you see in the picture, Danny?
   Student[1]: Dick.
   Student[2]: Pete and Dick.
   Student[3]: Pete and Dick.
   Teacher: What do they have?
   [9(1) M1   896]

Third, while ellipsis is common in the students' speech, when *they* are building on the teacher's speech, it is much less common in the teacher's speech, at least at the first-grade level. However, teacher *expansion* of the child's often elliptical speech is a very common form of *ratification*, and it is a common device for incorporating the child's utterance into the teacher's utterance.

8. *Teacher:*   Remember ____ who's using his imagination now?
   Student: Daddy.
   Teacher: Daddy's using his imagination and he's telling part of
                  the same story that Mark is telling . . . .
   [6(1) WS1–126]

9. *Teacher:*   Jim, what's Sally doing with the wagon?
   Student[1]: Push/in it/.
   Student[2]: /Pushin/it for mother.
   Teacher: She's pushing it to mother, isn't she, so mother will be
                  safe.
   [9(1) M1–828]

A fourth way in which teachers ratify student speech is by simple repetition of part or all of the child's response.

10. *Teacher:*   It's something you do every year until you get as/big as
                  you're going to get./
    Student[s]: /Grow. Grow/Grow.
    Teacher: Grow. Right.
    [7(1) WS1–38]

11. *Teacher:*   . . . . They're on their way to what?
    Student[s]: Ocean. Pacific Ocean
    Teacher: Ocean. Yes.
    Student: Ocean.
    [8(2) M1–498]

This characterization of ratification is not comprehensive. Rather, it identifies some of the most *common* ways in which teachers verbally acknowledge and incorporate students' utterances into their own.

Teachers also *fail to ratify* the utterances of students in several common ways, singly and in combination.

First, teachers sometimes directly reject the utterances of the children, particularly when questioning them to determine their grasp of curriculum materials:

12. *Teacher*:   Is that what he said to the someone? "I whizzed around and around?"
    Student: Yeh.
    Teacher: No, that isn't what he said to the someone. Find the words that tell what he said to the someone.
    [6(1) WS1–997]

13. *Teacher*:   Now without being silly think of something that does not smell good.
    Student: Skunk.
    Teacher: Now, don't name *that* one again. O.K.
    [7(2) WS1–826]

Sometimes the teachers indicate a lack of ratification by providing a correct response where the student has given no response or an unacceptable response. Such modification is sometimes similar to the expansion of acceptable responses discussed earlier, and both sorts of responses can accordingly be ambiguous in intent.

14 *Teacher*:   The lark what to the tree?
   Student: Song.
   Teacher: *Flew to the tree*. It's a bird. It flew to the tree.
   [6(1) WS1–55]

It is also common for teachers to indicate nonincorporation of students' utterances by repetition of their own previous utterance.

Repetition of one's own utterance, where there has been *no* response from the person addressed, is widespread in verbal interaction. We hear it in the classroom, from both teacher *and* student.

15. *Teacher*:   What would he say if he were surprised? (   )
    What would the spaceman say if he were surprised to see Mark?
    [6(1) WS1–150]

16. *Teacher*:   Does that sound like he's surprised? He said to Mark, "What made you so slow? Does that sound like he's surprised?"

   [6(1) WS1–203]

17. *Teacher*:   Write your name, but don't make any other marks on this paper.

   Student: (Write) our last name? Miz Thomas, write our last name?

   [6(2) WS1–894]

The repetition here indicates that the repeater has not heard anything that can be interpreted as a response. But, there is also such repetition from the teacher when an utterance from a student *can* be heard and interpreted as an answer to the teacher. When this occurs, we must infer that the teacher has not heard what we have heard, or is rejecting the response as inappropriate:

18. *Teacher*:   The last one says the lark _____ did what to the tree. The lark _____.

   Student: Ate.

   Teacher: The lark what to the tree?

   [6(1) WS1–55]

19. *Teacher*:   Let's look now at number—eleven. Can you read that for us/ /uh, Les?

   Student[1]:   /Yes./

   Teacher: Can you find the (letters) for us and read it?

   Student[2]:   Salmon—Salmon.

   Student[3]:   I can read it.

   Student[2]:   Salmon eggs (   ).

   Teacher: I don't hear Les. Les count eleven. Look down at eleven . . . .

   [8(2) M1–498]

The repetition has the effect of holding the interaction in place. The teacher will not move the action forward until its elements are properly constituted. This process essentially involves cycling back through a segment of interaction. Schegloff (1972) has identified such recycling as evidence that a conversation is being repaired.[4]

From this discussion, it should be evident that while the turn economies and the participant structures are designed to equalize students' access to the floor, the teacher's response patterns are not. Instead, the teacher s response patterns *selectively incorporate* student's utterances heard and judged to be appropriate or correct, and ignore those that are incorrect and inappropriate. Thus, when we

consider not just who spoke, but who was heard and *verbally* defined by the teacher as having contributed to the interaction, it is
apparent that some children's speech may be ratified more often
than others.

This basic ratification process is the heart of the children's learning experience. It is the teacher's primary means for letting the children know when they are responding as she thinks they should. At
the same time, there can be many reasons for the absence of ratification, which the teacher does not always articulate. Thus, children
must somehow be able to make inferences from the patterning in the
teacher's ratification and nonratification that will inform them as to
what sorts of mistakes they are making.[5]

The Student Infrastructure

From the teacher's point of view, both a failure to respond and inappropriate responses from students are due in part to student inattention when the teacher is speaking.

The control of students' focus of attention is a very salient concern for the teacher. The focuses of attention designated for the students by the teacher (usually either desk work or her own talk) are
those thought to provide the knowledge that schools purport to
teach. If a child is "properly" focused, it is still not certain he is
learning, since he may be thinking about or selectively attending to
signaling sources other than those his behavior gives evidence he is
attending to. But, if the student is improperly focused, then it is certain, from the teacher's point of view, that he is *not* learning.

In practice improper focus (from the teacher's point of view)
usually involves students' paying attention to one another rather
than to the teacher or to their desk work. Students are typically
allowed self-control in initiating and sustaining encounters with
other students only during periods when teacher control is lifted, or
in other words during recesses. While there is a sense in which a return to the classroom signals the suspension of this children's world,
with its own system of assumptions and rules for conveying attention and regulating talk, the relationships among the children do not
disappear.

Interaction between children can occur at almost any time during official classroom interaction, but it flourishes wherever the
teacher's attention is not focused. When she is engaged in interaction with a small group or a single student, those students outside
her involvement, whose attention should be focused on desk work,
are more likely to become engaged in interaction with one another

than those within her encounter. Yet even within her encounter those who are not being directly addressed or attended to by the teacher are more likely to become involved with one another than those being directly addressed.

Mutual involvement between students also increases during the junctures or transition points when one interactional arrangement is being terminated and another initiated. It is also common among students who are waiting for the teacher to tell them how to allocate their involvement while she is in the process of giving instructions to others.

Interaction among children that is initiated, sustained, and controlled by them differs markedly from the official interaction controlled by the teacher. Rather than one person allocating involvement and regulating the talk, all potential parties to a student interaction contribute to the joint sustaining of interaction. Speakers attempt to attract the attention of hearers and to designate those they want to have attend to them. Those whose attention they seek have the choice of attending or disattending, of assuming the position of hearer and validating the speech of another or ignoring it.

Children speaking to one another in the classroom communicate in a manner that is inherently less attention attracting than when they are outside during recess in order to avoid attracting the teacher's attention. First graders quickly learn to whisper, and to visually monitor the teacher to make sure that she is in fact not attending to them when they are talking to each other.

Teachers vary in the extent to which they attempt to prevent and stop interaction between students. The degree to which students' attention is allocated in ways designated by the teacher is sometimes used as a measure of the degree of control a teacher exercises over her students. It is also sometimes used as a measure of the teacher's ability to maintain students' interest in the curriculum materials she presents, and hence as a measure of her teaching abilities. Teachers who wish to sustain a controlled and orderly classroom, rather than one which is relaxed and casual, endeavor to minimize the amount of interaction between students.

Teachers also vary in the extent to which they attempt to co-opt infrastructure interaction and integrate it into the official structure. Students are sometimes allowed to sit next to those with whom they prefer to engage in interaction, if they can limit the amount of interaction they have with their peers, or maintain such interaction without attracting the attention of the teacher and disrupting official interaction to a degree unacceptable to the teacher. Children who engage in too much interaction with one another are physically separated, or positioned so that talk between them is made difficult.

All teachers, however, are concerned that such peer involvements do not reach a level of frequency that prevents the students from attending to the communication through which curriculum material is transmitted.

At the same time, children are not held fully accountable for lapses of attention in ways that adults are. It is understood that the younger the child is, the shorter his attention span will be. And while schools assume that a child entering school will already have acquired certain types of interactional competence, teachers understand that it will be necessary in the early grades for them to teach the children how to behave in a manner that is socially appropriate for the maintenance of official classroom interaction.

Learning How to Get the Floor in the Classroom

At the first-grade level, teachers devote considerable time and considerable explicit verbal instruction to teaching their students how to behave in ways that convey they are attending to the teacher. Considerable time is also devoted to teaching children how to take turns at talk in an orderly fashion. The teacher tells the students when their level of physical activity is too great. She directs them in how to position themselves in relation to others, and provides detailed information on appropriate body alignment and posture (e.g., "sit up straight," "put your feet on the floor," "don't turn sideways in your desk"). She also explicitly tells the students to look at her when she is speaking. And whenever the students are behaving in ways that suggest inattention, the teachers directs them to pay attention.

In regard to the regulation of talk, the teacher's main concern is that the children learn the classroom systems for the allocation of student turns at talk. In the first grade, students often talk while others are talking, talk before the teacher has designated someone to talk, talk when the teacher has designated someone else to speak, and make verbal contributions that the teacher perceives as irrelevant to the discussion. All of these violations of the regulation of student turns are explicitly addressed by the teacher, in directives such as "Don't talk when someone else is talking;" "Don't talk until I call on you;" "It's not your turn;" or "We're not talking about that right now."

As the children get older, they less frequently violate the rules for taking turns at talk, and the frequency of teacher directives to correct such violations also decrease so that the rules for regulating interaction become increasingly implicit. The students also become increasingly skillful in violating the rules for taking turns at talk in ways that will not be reprimanded by the teacher, a type of competence that will be discussed in more detail in the next chapter.

As they grow older, students also become more skillful in managing the infrastructure interaction among themselves that is not controlled by the teacher, without any instruction from their elders. In general, as they become older, they become capable of sustaining encounters for longer periods of time that involve larger numbers of people. At the first-grade level, a conversation between just two students is rarely sustained for more than five minutes, even when it is not terminated by the teacher. When a third person joins such an encounter, difficulties in taking turns at talk immediately arise, so that constantly more than one student is trying to speak at the same time. The participation of a fourth student almost invariably results in the breakdown of the encounter into two encounters. By the sixth grade, groups of four or five are capable of sustaining encounters for an indefinite period. Indian and Anglo students differ in their acquisition of such skills, in ways that will be discussed in the following chapter.

In general, then, students in the classroom learn not only the curriculum content that is transmitted through verbal interaction with the teacher, but also how to regulate interaction so that the transmission of such content can be accomplished. The systems for regulating talk in the *official* structuring of interaction are by and large designed to allocate turns in encounters involving large numbers of persons. Such encounters invariably entail a differentiation of participants through which one person allocates the positions of speaker and listeners among the others present. In addition, this differentiation of controller and controlled is institutionalized, or associated with specific roles that are themselves an aspect of the organization of the particular institution (in this case, an educational institution) within which interaction occurs.

But the systems that are used for regulating talk in the classroom, and the skill the students acquire in sustaining interaction through the use of such systems, do not become irrelevant when students leave the classroom. Rather, these systems for regulating talk serve as resources for organizing interaction in a wide variety of institutional frameworks in which the students will participate as adults—resources they will draw on again and again in later life.

In particular, the systems learned in the classroom are used for organizing interaction among large numbers of people in the occupational world that most eventually enter. This world, like the classroom, is typically organized into hierarchies of positions which have associated with them the same kind of differentiation of interactional prerogatives that distinguish teacher and student in the classroom. Thus, at business meetings, it is the "boss" who regulates the employees turns at talk, much as the teacher controls student talk. It is the boss who allocates the employees' attention and attempts to insure that their attention remains focused on productive work activity, rather than being diverted to involvements that are not a part of the official organization of work. So the teacher socializes students in skills for regulating interaction that prepare them for the occupational world they will enter as adults, and for the organization of interaction through which they maintain working relations with others in that world.

The roles of teacher and student are partially conveyed through the *institutionalized* classroom system for regulating interaction that has been described. At the same time, other dimensions of social reality *emerge* through the interactional process so that Indian and Anglo students emerge as very differently defined social beings. The next chapter deals with the differences.

Notes

1 Philips (1974b) provides a more detailed discussion of some of the inherent differences between written and spoken communication.
2. Even though the small-group arrangement leaves those not in the group at their desks, they still spend less time focused on individual desk work than the sixth graders do.
3. See Appendix A for notational devices used in transcription.
4. The teachers' use of repair techniques to instruct the children makes it clear that although it is the teacher's own utterance that is being repeated, the teacher can rarely be said to be engaged in self-correction.
5. This general concept of ratification was first developed in Philips (1974a: 162–183), with the intent to relate teachers' ratification of students' utterances to a more general view of ratification in face-to-face interaction. The discussion of specific forms of ratification and non-ratification, and the transcript examples are new to this revision and to Philips (1981). Mehan's (1979) concept of the three turn unit basic to the lesson, based on his and Courtney Cazden's 1974–75 classroom research, is similar, except for the notion that a unit is involved, and the notion that the behavior identified is lesson-specific, rather than characteristic of all interaction.

7

A Comparison of Indian and Anglo Communicative Behavior in Classroom Interaction

The purpose of this chapter is to compare Indian and Anglo students' behavior in the classroom within the framework of the organization of classroom interaction laid out in Chapter 6. We will ask how the students differ and consider the implications of those difference for the Indian children's learning experience.

Such differences are of practical concern primarily because Indian children do not seem to be learning as much in the classroom as Anglo children do. We will first consider the main sources of evidence that Indian students are not comprehending the material presented in classroom lessons. The rest of the chapter is then both an elaboration and an explanation of that evidence. Ultimately the learning difficulties are traced to cultural differences between Indian and Anglo systems of communication in face-to-face interaction.

Evidence of Indian Noncomprehension in the Classroom

School district personnel and tribal officials have been aware for some time that Warm Springs Indian students do not do well on national achievement tests that measure comprehension and retention of school curriculum. That pattern is in keeping with the general pattern for reservation Indian students, who generally fall below the national norms on such measures. Discussion of such test results, however, often focuses on the possibility that they do not accurately reflect the knowledge of students from ethnic minority backgrounds because the test-taking experience itself is best adapted to the cultural background of students who are Anglo and middle class. Minority students are in this way handicapped as test takers. While this may in fact be true, such discussion tends to distract attention from what actually goes on in the classroom. The point I wish to make here is that one need not turn to test results for evidence of Indian students' difficulties in comprehending school curriculum. Such difficulty is painfully evident in the day-to-day exchange of talk between teacher and students, particularly when all-Indian and all-Anglo classes are contrasted.

There are three major sources of evidence of Indian students' lack of comprehension of teacher talk that I wish to deal with here. First, Indian students at both the first- and sixth-grade levels talk less than their Anglo peers in official classroom interaction controlled by the teacher. Most notably, Indian students respond less often to the questions posed by the teacher to determine whether the students understand the curriculum material.

The teachers in the Warm Springs grade school directed my attention to the lesser amount of talk among Indian students. The most common view among the teachers was that the Indian children talked a good deal until around the time they entered the fourth grade. At that time there was thought to be a marked decrease in the amount of talk by the Indian students in official classroom interaction.

My own observations indicated that even at the first-grade level, Indian students responded to the teacher less than their Anglo counterparts. Nevertheless, it was also true that Indian first graders talked much more than Indian sixth graders.

The commonness of an absence of response from Indian first graders identified individually to directions given and questions asked even prompted me to inquire into their hearing ability, but there was no evidence of hearing loss for any of the children being observed in results of the hearing tests regularly given to the students.

It is true that a failure to respond cannot automatically be taken as evidence of noncomprehension. But in practice that inference is made. And minimally it is clear that the teacher cannot determine whether the students understand what she has said and know how to respond appropriately, if they do not respond at all.

A second source of evidence of greater noncomprehension on the part of Indian students was the greater frequency with which the responses they *did* make were defined as inappropriate by the teacher through her failure to ratify what they said in her responses to them.

In Chapter 6, I discussed some of the various ways in which a teacher can ratify or fail to ratify a student's response to something she says. We tend to think of the teacher as helping the students distinguish right and wrong answers, as in the following exchange:

1. *Teacher*: (reading) "Long ago campers were like ____"
   Student[1]: This.
   Student[2]: That.
   Teacher: Something that starts like ____ with T.
   Students: (New   ). (Truck). Camper. Old truck. Cheaper. Camper. Like camping.
   Teacher: /(What is)/ this on the back of the truck?
   Student: /(   )/
   Students: Tent. Tent.
   Teacher: Alright, (continues reading) "Long ago campers were like tents." It starts with a T. "Now they are like homes." If you were going camping, would you rather sleep in a tent or a camper?

   [7(2) WS1–626]

In this exchange there is only one right answer to the question the teacher has posed, since she is reading from a *Weekly Reader* and asking the children to read a word.

There are, however, judgments other than the right and wrong sort being made in the teacher's responses to the students:

2. *Teacher*: . . . . Now without being silly/   /think of something that does not smell good.
   Student[1]: /(It's not)/
   Student[2]: Skunk!
   Teacher: Now don't name *that* one again. O.K.
   Student[2]: Skunk.
   Teacher: (It looks like you got ____) O.K. We were/(thinking of)/ things now.
   Student[3]: /A lion./
   Student[4]: One of those/(one things)/.
   Teacher: /What else/doesn't?
   Student[3]: A lion.
   Teacher: Well, where did you smell a lion?
   Student[3]: (   ) one time we went on a trip and there's a (real) lion and uh (we) went to Africa and then I smelled one (of them real lions) and it stinked.

> *Teacher*:   Now, Lee, (alright) we said we weren't gonna be silly.
> We were gonna really name some things that do not
> smell good without being silly.
>
> [7(2) WS1–826]

In this piece of discourse the teacher's rejection of skunk and lion as responses to the question, "What does not smell good?" is based on something other than the factual inaccuracy of those responses, for in fact both animals do smell sometimes.

In some cases the teacher's failure to ratify a student's utterance is due to her inability to comprehend what the student is saying:

> 3. *Teacher*:   Alright. Larry? Why would you rather sleep in a
> camper than a tent?
> *Student*[1]:   Cause if you sleep in a tent all the animals can get in.
> *Student*[2]:   (   )
> *Teacher*:   What?
> *Student*[2]:   (Cause it will scare you).
> *Teacher*:   It will scare you?
> *Student*:   Somebody might.
> *Teacher*:   Oh, somebody might scare you if you were in the tent.
> Do you think they could scare you if you were in the
> camper?
>
> [7(2) WS1–626]

Here the teacher appears to have difficulty identifying what "it" refers to in the student's response, "Cause it will scare you." The student's way of trying to build on prior discourse is not comprehensible to the teacher, and so she has no way of ratifying what the student has said in a meaningful fashion, until he modifies his utterance. Here we can say that the teacher is teaching discourse skills, although this type of teaching is probably somewhat less conscious than efforts to get children to correctly identify the meaning of words they are reading.

In the three examples of teacher nonratification, the teacher is addressing a range of language skills in her responses to the children.

Thus far I have talked about Indian student nonresponsiveness and the greater infrequency of teacher ratification of student utterances as sources of evidence from which one can infer that Indian children are comprehending less than their Anglo peers. A third source of evidence of Indian students' relative noncomprehension is the frequency with which they ask questions in response to the teacher's instructions. Their questions suggest they are very uncertain about their own comprehension.

Indian students in the sixth grade do not give expression to this uncertainty about what it is they are supposed to be doing in front of their peers (i.e., during interaction involving the whole class or a small group). They save it for the one-to-one encounters with the teacher on which they rely very heavily for clarification. But at the first-grade level, confusion and uncertainty are quite apparent:

4. *Teacher*:   Will you please take one dark color crayon on your desk. One dark color crayon.

   Student[1]:   (Bring) two?
   Student[2]:   Any color?
   Student[3]:   (   )
   Student[4]:   This color?
   Teacher: One *dark* color crayon. I'm going to give you another piece of paper ____ and ____ don't make any ____ write your name on the paper, but don't make any other marks on this paper.
   Student: (Write) our last name? Miz Carter, write our last name?
   [6(2) WS1 – 879-894]

5. *Teacher*:   Now (I'd) like for you to make four clocks.
   Student[1]:   /Miz Carter/
   Student[2]   /Miz Carter/
   Teacher: /Make four clocks./
   Students: (   )
   Teacher: I'll show you.
   Student[3]:   With a pencil?
   Student: With a pen?
   Teacher: With your color crayon.
   [6(2) WS1 – 948-961]

The students also ask one another these same kinds of questions.

Usually, in asking both the teacher and one another these questions, the students are in violation of the rules for talk regulation within official classroom interaction. More often than not the questions the children pose are not asked during periods when the floor is open to students for that purpose. Rather, they occur as the teacher continues to give instructions or turns her attention elsewhere.

Some of the questions are answered, some are not. The Indian students never get all of their questions answered by the teacher, nor for that matter do the Anglo students, although they have fewer such questions. Teachers are oriented toward operating on a point-time basis. They are obliged to accomplish a certain number of lessons within a given period of time, in keeping with a study plan. They must constantly make choices between the learning needs of the individual and the group as a whole. Thus the choice is made regularly to ignore some individuals' questions in order to expose the class as a whole to more curriculum material.

In time the students turn more and more to their peers for answers to such questions. Indian students turn to their peers more than Anglo students do. By the sixth grade neither Anglo nor Indian students ask many questions requesting clarification of instructions in the presence of their peers. However, the Indian students in the sixth grade do continue to use the opportunity for one-to-one encounters with the teacher to pose such questions, and do so much more frequently than the non-Indian students.

Thus far I have considered several types of evidence that suggest the Warm Springs Indian children do not comprehend as much of what the teacher is trying to communicate as the Anglo children do. At the same time, it is important to bear in mind that noncomprehension is itself a negotiated social reality. Such labeling ignores the fact that the teacher does not comprehend the Indian children's efforts to communicate to her any better than they understand her. The focus here is on the Indian children because they are the ones who will suffer in the long run because they do not understand.

It is also important to point out that there are not necessarily individual teachers or students to be blamed for the students' lack of understanding. The purpose of the rest of this chapter is to discuss some of the ways in which the Indian students' behavior, both as listeners and as speakers, can be explained by their culturally distinctive early socialization.

Paying Attention in the Classroom

Teachers are understandably concerned that their students pay attention to whatever focus of attention they designate. If students do not attend to the messages designed to instruct them, then they will not learn.

Teachers frequently reprimand students who are not paying attention, particularly at the first-grade level, and Indian students are reprimanded more often than non-Indian students for not paying attention. Thus the possibility arises that Indian students are comprehending less because they are not paying attention.

In this section I will discuss several reasons why Indian students are perceived and defined by the teacher through interaction as relatively inattentive. First, the Indian children convey attention in different ways than Anglo children, and so may be attending when the teacher thinks they are not. In other words, their listening behavior is culturally distinctive. Second, Indian children really do pay less attention to their teachers than the Anglo children do. This is partly because the Indian children are more involved with and interested in interaction with their schoolmates. But there is also evidence of a tuning out of the general evironment which suggests that something beyond peer involvement is involved. Each of these reasons for the impression that Indian students are less attentive will now be considered in more detail.

The Listening Behavior Is Different

When the teacher is talking in official interaction that she controls, Indian students' behavior as listeners differs from that of Anglo students in ways that hold true for both first and sixth graders.

The Indian students do not look at the teacher as much of the time as non-Indian students do. Their gaze is away from the teacher's face more of the time that she is speaking. They also spend more of the time that the teacher is speaking gazing at one another.

Indian students also provide fewer of the back channel signals that Anglos typically rely upon for evidence that their talk is being attended to. The Indian students nod in agreement with what the teacher is saying less than the Anglo students. They contribute fewer expressions of enthusiasm such as "Yay," "O boy," and clapping when the teacher announces plans to carry out activities like story reading, free time, and field trips, that the children are thought to particularly enjoy. The Indian children also interject fewer comments during teacher talk that demonstrate their having heard what she has said.

Some of the behavior that teachers consider to be evidence of inattention can be attributed to the cultural differences in the ways that Warm Springs Indians convey attention that were discussed in Chapter 4. Warm Springs Indians generally look at one another less when engaged in conversation, and generally provide less back channel signaling. They are unaccustomed to the domination and control of talk by a single individual. They are inclined to distribute their attention more equally among all those who are party to a given focused encounter.

Indian Children Pay More Attention to Their Peers

In addition, Warm Springs Indian children generally spend more time engaged in infrastructure interaction with their peers than the Anglo children in Madras, and the quality of that interaction is quite distinctive, particularly at the first-grade level.

Among Indian first graders there is more interaction involving use of the visual and tactile channels of communication. When the Indian children are engaged in interaction, they signal to one another through gestures and body movements, often to try to make others laugh. This can involve wide-ranging and inventive movements. They open their eyes very wide, move their heads in unusual patterns, and make faces at one another. They show one another things, directing attention to a torn shirt, an untied shoe, a funny picture, a crayon held between the fingers in an odd manner. Often too they imitate one another. Thus if one child squats on his chair and the teacher tells him not to, a second child will immediately squat on his chair, while the two of them look at one another and giggle.

There is also more physical contact involved in the interaction of first-grade Indian students. Most of it is of a teasing nature. When standing in line they push and bump against each other more. While they are seated, one may trip another who is moving around the room, grap his arm in passing, or block his path with his desk. They poke each other and step on each other's feet. Sometimes they even end up wrestling on the floor.

They invade one another's territory. They hide each other's crayons and pencils. They mark and tear each other's papers so that assignments handed in have a mutilated appearance not seen in the non-Indian students' papers. In the cafeteria, one will take food off another's plate when he isn't looking, put it on the plate of a third child, and then blame the third child for the act.

In all of this play one sees a good deal of faking and pretense, or creating a sense that things are other than they "really" are. Thus one sees students pretending to fall out of their chairs, pretending to be in pain, ramming into others and then pretending surprise they were there, all usually, but not always, belied by laughter that follows the pretense. The children deny hiding things, moving food, and marking papers, and blame others: "He did it." This is the substance of what ethnographers refer to as the "teasing" that is said to be prevalent among North American Indian societies (Philips, 1975a). The children do not always laugh about it. They sometimes become angry and tell each other, "Stop bothering me," or tell the teacher that a certain one is teasing them.

In the sixth grade the Indian students are much more settled. They sit and stand in a manner judged appropriate by the teacher. They still continue to signal to one another nonverbally across greater distances, but do not imitate one another in the same way. The physical contact continues to be greater than among Anglos, but it is more covert. While the students are poking or pushing one another, while one presses the foot of another, they seem to be ignoring one another. The territorial invasions continue, but are much reduced in frequency. The teasing by pretense and fakery continues, but it is done more in a verbal mode. Students tell one another things that aren't true, and say things about one another to others than aren't true—as when one student tells the teacher another student has done something the student isn't supposed to do that the student hasn't done at all.

The teachers at the first-grade level are more censorious of physical activity than they are of verbal activity. Physical activity is treated by the teacher as more disruptive. It is as if some talk at this age is viewed as inevitable, whereas physical containment and control are expected. Some teachers invoke age-competency expectations—e.g., "You're too big for that;" "Act your age;" in scolding students. They also invoke the disruptiveness of actions as a basis for censoring them: "We can't work if you do that;" "You're bothering your neighbors."

It is difficult to determine how much censoring Indian students is due to their greater amount of involvement with their peers, and how much is due to the fact that their involvement is generally of a qualitatively different sort.

One implication of the teacher's scolding is that it implies the notion that physical activity is more inherently distracting and disruptive than talk, for the people engaged in it or for their peers. But this is problematic. The notion that physical activity is more disruptive entails assumptions about what people must screen or exclude from one channel of communication (i.e., the visual channel) for the effective use of another channel (i.e., the auditory channel). Such assumptions in turn entail additional assumptions about how people can effectively combine different modes and channels of communication. Those assumptions tend to be viewed as if they were based on inherent human capacities rather than on culturally learned usages. Yet the discussion of channel use in Chapter 4 makes it clear that the Indian children's greater use of the visual and tactile channels is consistent with the early emphasis on use of the visual channel in the socialization of Warm Springs Indian children.

It should be apparent from this discussion that defining Indian children as inattentive is partly due to cultural differences in signaling attention. It is also partly due to the fact that Indian children really do pay less attention to the teacher and more to their peers. And finally, it is also due to the fact that the type of attention Indians devote to their peers is culturally different from that of Anglo students, and hence more likely to be noticed by the teacher and defined as inappropriate.

The Disintegration of Attention

There are other differences in the behavior of Indian and Anglo students that are evident at the first-grade level only. These cannot so readily be explained in terms of cultural differences. First, Indian students in the first grade are generally much more physically active than their Anglo counterparts, even when they are not involved with their peers. While this greater degree of physical activity is evident in a variety of circumstances, it is particularly evident when they are being addressed as a group by the teacher and are supposed to be paying attention. When they are seated in chairs they sit sideways, slip off the chairs and under the table, squat on the chairs, occasionally stand on them, and while seated lean over to touch the floor with their hands and even their heads. When seated on the floor, they lie on it, lean on it on their elbows, and slide across it. In sum, they engage in movement that violates classroom norms for appropriate body posture while listening much more of the time than do Anglo students.

As was mentioned earlier, Indian first graders also more often give no evidence whatsoever of having heard talk that is directed toward them by the teachers. In addition, during teacher talk, as well as at other times, Indian students use their bodies and their voices to produce a number of sounds that the teacher censors. They drum on the floor with their hands and feet when sitting on it. At their desks they tap their pencils and slam their desk lids. With their voices they make bird calls and repetitious sound patterns—e.g., chugga-chugga-chugga, du-du-du-du. These vocalizations occur most often when the Indian students are working alone at their desks, but they also occur occasionally while the teacher is talking; and whenever a student is vocalizing in this way, that student is much less likely than usual to respond to the teacher's talk.

These particular aspects of first-grade Indian children's behavior cannot all readily be explained by simple direct reference to the students' cultural background. As indicated in Chapter 5, Indian children develop the ability to sit quite still at much younger ages than Anglo children, so one cannot argue that their high level of physical activity is due to some kind of culturally acquired inability to sit still. However, in the Indian community, the emphasis on socialization for physical control entails an alternation between active control—expressed in play, in athletics, and in dance—and calm control—

expressed in the aforementioned ability to sit still when party to adult verbal interaction.

In practice, classroom interaction rarely provides the opportunity for or fosters the expression of either type of control. The development of active physical control is allocated to physical education sessions and recess on the playground. And although first-grade teachers occasionally introduce games that require physical activity in the classroom (for example, playing a record that directs students to raise their arms, stand on one foot, turn around in a circle, and so on), such activities occur infrequently, and do not really call for the types of control in motion that Indian children have developed.

While first-grade teachers' constant exhortations to students to sit down and sit up straight might be taken as evidence of an intent to develop calm control among their students, the standards for what constitutes calmness in students' classroom behavior differ considerably from those maintained in Indian community contexts.

Teachers tolerate and even encourage a much higher level of verbal excitation in the classroom than is acceptable in Warm Springs community contexts. This is because they interpret the active back channel verbalization of the Anglo students as evidence of interest, attention, and enthusiasm for what they have to say.

Teachers even try to encourage more back channel verbalizations by altering the pitch and intensity of their voices, much as parents do with babies (Blount, 1972). In other words, teachers often make an effort to increase the level of students' verbal excitation and to associate that increase with greater involvement in the learning process.

But physical excitation is not encouraged by the teacher. Many Anglo students express their desire to be called on by standing up at their desks as they strain to attract the teacher's eye to their frantically waving hands, but this is as far as they may go. Movement that alters proper body alignment so that the child is no longer facing the teacher, or movement that takes the child outside the personal space defined by his or her own desk is subject to verbal reprimand by the teacher.

Thus whereas both verbal and physical excitation suggesting a lack of control are discouraged in the Warm Springs community, in the classroom verbal excitation is encouraged but physical excitation is discouraged. The Indian children who are unaccustomed to the classroom pattern are allowed by the teacher to become overly excited (by community standards) from too little opportunity for controlled physical activity and too much opportunity for out-of-control verbal activity.

The greater frequency with which Indian first graders show no sign of having heard talk directed to them, and produce a number of noises that decrease the likelihood of their hearing what the teacher is saying, cannot readily be explained by cultural differences either. These behaviors were never evident in the interaction of young Warm Springs children in Warm Springs community situations.

It seemed plausible to hypothesize that some of the nonhearing and noise making might be a deliberate rejection of the teacher's authority in the classroom. Such rejection was clearly evident in the explicit pressure that is brought to bear on Indian high school students who excel in their school work by their peers, who see such performance as a type of selling out, or becoming Anglo. As McDermott has pointed out:

> A significant number of what are usually described as reading disabilities represent *situationally induced inattention patterns* which make sense in terms of the politics of the interethnic classroom. Pariah children learn not to read as one way of acquiring high status and strong identity in a host classroom. (McDermott, 1974:83)

It is likely that the noises which Indian children produce are sometimes a deliberate rejection of teacher authority. On more than one occasion when a student was reprimanded for slamming his desk lid, the reprimand was immediately followed by the slamming of several more desk lids in rapid succession, and this pattern was not limited to desk lids. However, it is unlikely that all of the actions in question were of this nature. I have already discussed how the mutual noncomprehension between student and teacher results in the students' actions being defined as inappropriate by the teacher. McDermott suggests that in classrooms where teacher and students have different communicative codes, the students adapt "by shutting down their attention skills" (1974:83). In this case, it is possible that the Warm Springs children are not only shutting down their attention skills, but also replacing scrambled sensory input with their own self-controlled sources of stimulation in the form of patterned noises.

Teachers' responses to what they perceive as inattention on the part of students are the same in both Indian and non-Indian classrooms, except that these responses occur more often in Indian classes, at least at the first-grade level. As indicated earlier, one response is to try harder to elicit more back channel work from the students by speaking louder and/or in a higher pitch range. Teachers also repeat what they have already said when they feel their addressees were not listening the first time.

It is also common to see teachers fix their gaze on the individuals who appear no to be attending until they realize that they are being stared at, and attempt to modify their behavior in order to be relieved of this gaze. And as already noted, children are also verbally reprimanded. In these ways the teacher more often than not singles out individuals one at a time for negative sanction rather than disciplining the group as a whole.

It seems likely that such teacher responses contribute to the uncertainty and confusion experienced by Indian students in classroom interaction, for in one way or another these responses are in conflict with the methods of discipline used by Warm Springs Indians in the care of children. As indicated in Chapter 5, voice loudness is generally not as great in Indian interactions, and increase in volume is not often used to convey greater intensity or to attract attention. Fixedness of gaze is associated with hostility of much greater intensity than among Anglos. In assigning blame and punishment, it is the group, not the individual, that is held responsible. And where only one child is involved, the discipline is usually provided privately, and outside the receiving range of others. Some high school student looking back on the grade school experience described the uncertainty such unfamiliar disciplinary tactics generate in this way:

6. *Student A*: I remember sometimes if you did something bad . . . then the teacher'd get mad and, like jerk 'em around . . . And then when you do something good, they'll come out, and—you know—"Who did that?" And everyone would get really scared and you just sit there and no one would answer. She goes, "That's really nice," you know? 'Cause you'd think she was gonna get mad at you for doing it. That's what I thought . . .

7. *Student B*: When I went to junior high, it was hard for me to read, 'cause in grade school I was too scared to read . . . because just like—said, that in grade school you were taught, "Be quiet and listen," you know? And then they'd want you to answer and if you was quiet, they'd get mad at you anyway. So, you know, you was all mixed up, unless you was teacher's pet or something. [VT1]

Teachers in the Warm Springs school who are sensitive to the students' reactions to such disciplinary responses to the inattention have, over time, modified their responses to be more in keeping with Indian cultural expectations. In the classrooms where I observed this to have taken place, the rapport with the students was very good.

In addition, by the sixth grade, all of the "inattentive" behavior that distinguishes Indian and non-Indian first graders—the high level of physical activity, the absence of response to teachers' verbal elicitations, and the noise making—have disappeared. By the age of eleven, the children have come to understand more of the communicative behavior of the teacher, and both Indian and non-Indian students are far more skilled in faking attention and in concealing inattention.

Thus some differences between Indian and Anglo students' communicative behavior as listeners are cultural differences both in behavior and the ways in which behavior is interpreted. But other distinguishing features of Indian student interaction, specifically at the first-grade level, occur no more often in the Indian community than they do in the Anglo classroom or community, and in all likelihood would be judged as inappropriate by Indian adults, just as they are so judged by Anglo teachers. Yet in spite of there being no direct equivalent to these features in Indian community contexts, I have argued here that even behavior that is unfamiliar in Indian contexts may be indirectly due to cultural differences in communicative behavior that create confusion in the child's mind sufficient to produce behavior defined as inappropriate by either set of cultural norms.

Direct evidence of a conflict for Indian children between culturally different systems of interaction is even more apparent in their speaking behavior.

Getting the Floor in the Classroom

Indian students generally make less effort than Anglo students to get the floor in classroom interaction. They compete with one another less for the teacher's attention, and make less use of the classroom interactional framework to demonstrate academic achievement. In the discussion to follow, these differences are described in detail, and related to the culturally distinctive adult organization of interaction and socialization of children described in Chapters 4 and 5.

Competing for the Floor

In the Anglo classrooms there is a general sense that students are constantly competing for the teacher's attention which does not exist in the Indian classrooms. One reason for this is that Indian students do not make efforts to get the floor as much as Anglo students do. I have already discussed the point that Indian students do not engage in as much back channel provision of evidence that they are attending to the teacher. The Indian students consequently cannot be said to select themselves as the teacher's listeners as much. Thus, to the degree that a student addressed by the teacher is more likely than other students to become the next speaker, Indian students make less use of this device for selecting themselves in this way.

In addition, when the teacher reaches those junctures in her own talk where she is preparing to turn the floor over to a student by calling on one, fewer Indian students raise their hands to be called on. And they do not verbally beg to be called on in the way that Anglo students do. Indian students also much more often do not respond at all when they are called upon, even when their behavior indicates they are paying attention.

Talking out of Turn

In addition to the Indian disinclination to select themselves as next speaker, Indian students also violate the rules for taking turns at talk less often than Anglo students. But this statement requires some clarification.

In the first grade, the Indian students take longer to learn the rules the teacher imposes to regulate their turns at talk. Especially in the early months of school, Indian children more often fail to raise their hands when directed to do so, and call out answers instead. Although the Anglo first graders adapt to the system faster, there are always some Anglo students who seem to be engaged in selective violation of the rules regulating student turns at talk—i.e., some of the time they follow the rules and some of the time they don't. They sometimes answer before the teacher has finished verbalizing a question:

8. *Teacher*: Do you think mother and father will play /Hide and Go Seek?/
   Student[1]: /Yeh/
   Student[2]: /Yeh./
   Student[3]: I do.
   Teacher: Do you think so? . . . .
   [9(1) M1–770]

9. *Teacher*: Oh my, is mother going to make it or is Dick going to /get/ there first?

Student: Mot/her/.
Teacher: Let's find out. . . .
[9(1) M1–828]

10. *Teacher*: Pete wants to know how to get a fast ride? /Would/ you
underline /that?/
Student[1]: /No./
Student[2]: /Yes/.
[9(1) M1–896]

Anglo first graders more often call out answers before the
teacher has called on someone. They often also answer when the
teacher has called on or named someone else as the next speaker:

11. *Teacher*: Let's find out. Amy would you read?
Student[1]: "Sally said."
Amy: "Sally said. . . ."
[9(1) M1–828)

12. *Teacher*: Jim, what's Sally doing with the wagon?
Student[1]: Pus/hin it./
Jim: /Pushin/ it for mother.
[9(1) M1–828]

In addition, Anglo students, who have already had a turn to speak
in a context within which the teacher has made it clear that everyone
must have a turn before anyone can have a second turn, often raise
their hands to be called on and even verbally beg to be called on.
   The Anglo students also much more frequently initiate talk with
the teacher while she is talking, when she has not explicitly ended
her turn at talk, or turned the floor over to a student:

13. *Teacher*: You'll remember in September that—something told
the salmon that it was time to leave the little stream
where they had hatched. And to swim down the
stream down to the great big Columbia River.
Student[1]: On the /stairs/.
Teacher: /So/that's /what they/ are doing now and on the way
down . . . a bear tried to get some of the salmon.
Student[2]: A /big bear/.
[8(2) M1–498]

14. *Teacher*: (reading) "Then they swam up the coast of Washington." And here they are almost to the border of Canada
where my finger is now.
Student: Canada. That's where my brother is.

Teacher: (continues reading) "Under them the ocean became twenty, then thirty, then fifty fathoms, or three hundred feet deep."
8(2) M1–498]

In both Anglo and Indian classrooms some students violated the rules for turn taking more often than others, and certain students predictably violated the rules in certain ways and not others. Students labeled by teachers as both "leaders" and "problems" violated the rules for taking turns at talk more frequently than those children who were never spontaneously discussed by the teachers. The patterns of violation for the two labeled types were probably different, but it was difficult to record and analyze data on this source of variation in verbal behavior, so this generalization is speculative.

By the sixth grade, most types of speaking out of turn have disappeared among both Indian and Anglo students, in keeping with their generally increased skill in managing interaction. The one kind of violation that continues to be far more common among Anglo students is the interjection of comments into the middle of the teacher's talk. By this age, the Anglo students are actively engaged in attempting to exert control over teacher-student interactions, and succeed far more often in doing so than at the first-grade level. Indian students, however, do very little of this, providing further evidence of their relative lack of involvement in official classroom interactions.

The teachers' responses to students' talking out of turn vary considerably. Sometimes they ignore the violator, sometimes they scold, sometimes they simply acknowledge what has been said, and sometimes they build and elaborate upon it. There are a number of factors that affect the tactic taken by the teacher in response to violations, including the number of times the student in question, as well as other students, has already violated the rules in both the recent and distant past, the number of students talking out of turn at a given point, the amount of time the teacher has left that was allocated to complete a given lesson, and the mood of the teacher. It is consequently not easy to see clear-cut patterns in the teachers' responses to talking out of turn. It may appear from the preceding discussion that the Indian students come either to know or abide by the rules for getting the floor in the classroom better than the Anglo students, and in a rather limited sense this is true. Talking out of turn may also be viewed as another way in which a student may get the floor. As I have already indicated, some students are more successful than others at being attended to and ratified by the teacher when speaking out of turn.

In adult life too some people are more successful at getting the floor by talking out of turn. And the variable use of such means is closely tied up with Anglo organization of status differentiation. The Anglo students who talk out of turn and who are responded to variably by the teacher are learning through their exercise of turn-controlling devices when such devices will work and when they will not, when they will be accepted as appropriate, and when they will not. Because the Indian students use such devices very little, and do not go through the same trial-and-error process of discovering their acceptable use, they are less likely to develop the skills that in adulthood would enable them to use the communicative resources available for managing the Anglo system for the expression and interpretation of status differentiation.

Distribution of Student Turns at Talk

In addition to this difference between Indian and Anglo students in the frequency of occurrence of talking out of turn, there is also a difference in the pattern of distribution of student responses to teachers' elicitations in the whole class and in small groups in terms of: (1) the frequency with which students raise their hands to indicate they want to be called on to answer a question; (2) the rapidity with which they raise their hands to be called on when the teacher opens the floor; and (3) the frequency with which students produce responses that are ratified by the teacher and incorporated into the discourse.

In the Anglo classrooms there is considerable variation among students in the frequency with which they come to have the floor. Some students raise their hands more than others. Some raise their hands sooner than others. And some provide responses that are more often validated by the teacher. Moreover, these three aspects of getting the floor typically function together. In other words, those students who raise their hands most often are also the students who raise their hands sooner, and who are most often ratified by the teacher. For all these reasons, these students have more turns at talk than others do.

In addition, there is a correlation between the frequency of Anglo students' turns at talk and their performance on written measures of achievement such as exercises, exams, and national tests. Generally, those who raise their hands more and faster and whose responses are more often validated by the teacher are the ones who receive higher scores on written measures of competence. One can see this pattern emerging in the first-grade classes, and at the sixth-grade level it is clear-cut.

In sum, although there are occasional interesting exceptions to this pattern, one can generally determine which students are evaluated by the teacher as good students on the basis of both their performance as speakers and the teacher's responses to their speech in teacher-structured interactions. Thus, in spite of the institutionalization of equalization of student participation through the turn systems discussed in Chapter 6, participation is in fact made unequal through the joint actions of both teacher and students.

In the Indian classrooms, the situation is very different. It is generally the case that the turns at talk are more evenly distributed in Indian classrooms. At the first-grade level some Warm Springs students do raise their hands more often and sooner than others in responding to the teacher's questions. However, there is not as much variation among Indian first graders in these respects as there is among Anglo students. What variation there is is due among the Warm Springs children to the almost total nonparticipation of several students in classroom interaction structured by the teacher.

There is clearly, however, more validation by the teachers of some Warm Springs students' responses than there is of others. And there is a correlation between students' performance on written measures of achievement and validation of their responses by the teacher. Those whose responses are more often validated by the teacher are also those who perform well on written assignments. It is also the case that to some degree those who raise their hands more often and sooner score higher on written tests. However, the correlation here is not nearly as strong as it is among Anglo first graders. In the Indian classroom it was common for children who had demonstrated the ability to answer correctly a particular question in one instance to refrain from even trying to answer the same question the next time it was raised. Thus it was clear that even when they knew answers to questions they did not always try to get the floor.

At the sixth-grade level the evidence of a differentiation among Indian students in frequency of floor holding and the relation between frequency of floor holding and achievement on written tests had largely disappeared.

As was mentioned earlier, at the sixth-grade level there is much less talk to teachers by Indian students in front of their peers than at the first-grade level to begin with. With regard to what talk there is, there is little difference among the students in how often or how quickly they raise their hands, except that there are still a few who never raise their hands at all. Nor by this age are some students' responses clearly more often validated by the teacher than those of other students. Consequently, the talk of Indian sixth graders is more evenly distributed in every sense than that of Anglo students.

It should be evident from the preceding discussion that there is generally little or no relation between amount of talk ratified or un-ratified by Indian sixth graders and their written performances. The results of their exams indicated that the Indian sixth graders varied considerably in their comprehension of all subjects. Yet it was very difficult to predict who would do well on written assignments on the basis of verbal performance in the Indian classroom, whereas it was easy to make accurate predictions in the Anglo classroom. Neverthe-less, it was apparent to the Indian students themselves who compre-hended the assignments. The students who were getting good grades were approached much more often than others by their peers for help with assignments during periods when they were working alone at their desks.

In the Anglo classrooms, then, students are differentiated in the frequency of their responses to the teacher, and those who have the floor more often are also evaluated more highly on written assign-ments. By contrast, in the Indian classrooms, students are not differ-entiated in terms of their frequency of response to the teacher, and amount of talk cannot be correlated with performance on written assignments.

It will be useful at this point to summarize the ways in which the participation of Indian and Anglo students as speakers differs. First, Indian students generally participate less as speakers. Second, they do not select themselves as next speakers as much: they do not be-have in ways that indicate to the teacher that they wish to speak. Third, Indian students do not as often respond when they are expli-citly asked to speak by the teacher. Fourth, while the Indian stu-dents are slower to learn the rules for regulating turns at talk in the classroom, once they have acquired them they don't violate them as often by talking out of turn. To put it another way, the Indian stu-dents do not as often use interruption and speaking when another has been addressed as devices for getting the floor. Finally, talk is more evenly distributed among Indian students so that a greater fre-quency of turns at talk is not correlated with better performance on written assignments as it is in the Anglo classrooms.

A Cultural Account

In attempting to account for the differences between Anglo and Indi-an students' behavior as addressors, a number of possible sources or causes of such differences can be plausibly invoked within a framework that emphasizes cultural differences. Here I will argue that the differences which have been discussed are due primarily, although not entirely, to an incompatibility between Indian and Anglo systems for the regulation of turns at talk. For the Indian students, getting the floor in classroom encounters regulated in Anglo fashion requires them to behave in ways that run counter to expectations of socially appropriate behavior in the Warm Springs Indian community.

It will be useful at this point to review the Chapter 4 discussion of the ways in which Indian and Anglo regulation of speaker change differ, and to highlight the senses in which the regulation of turns at talk in the classroom are characteristic of Anglo organization of interaction.

Indian organization of interaction can be characterized as maximizing the control that an individual has over his or her own turn at talk, and as minimizing the control that a given individual has over the turns of others. This system of control is largely accomplished through three aspects of turn taking. First, address by a speaker is more often general, rather than focused on a particular individual. This minimizes the possibility that any single addressee can or will deprive the speaker of a floor by withdrawing attention. In addition, to the degree that focused address increases the likelihood that the person the speaker seeks as a listener will be the next speaker, general address eliminates this possibility.

Second, in Indian interaction an immediate response to what a speaker has said is not always necessary, but may be delayed. Long pauses between speakers' turns at talk are common, as are responses that occur after other topics have been pursued. This provides the potential respondent with more control in determining when to speak and whether to speak at all.

Finally, Indian speakers control the ends of their own turns; they are not interrupted by others.

Such features that maximize the speakers' control over their own turn at talk also allow for the potential abuse of the system, so that in theory a given speaker could run on and on without interruption. But in practice, talk is usually distributed equally among Indian parties to an encounter. In a given encounter some people may not talk at all, but the turns of those who *do* speak vary little in length and frequency.

By contrast, Anglo interaction may be characterized as involving greater exercise on the part of speakers and hearers of control over the turns of others. While address is by no means always directed to a single listener, focused address is much more common in Anglo interaction than in Indian interaction. Focused address allows the person addressed to control the speaker's turn by choosing to provide or withdraw attention. Because an addressed recipient is more likely to be the next speaker, focused address gives the speaker some control over who will speak next. Anglo interaction also normally entails the assumption that if a response to a speaker is going to occur, it will immediately follow the end of that speaker's turn at talk. This means the respondent has little control over the point at which she or he will reply. Finally, Anglo interaction is characterized by interruption of speakers that results in the ends of their turns being controlled by others. Moreover, it is not uncommon for two people to begin speaking at once in Anglo interactions, which in turn seems related to the absence of pause between speakers' turns at talk. While one speaker may defer to another, this event often allows those sought as listeners to choose between speakers through their allocation of attention.

In Anglo conversation where there is no institutionalized system for allocating turns at talk as there is in the classroom, all participants theoretically have access to the means for controlling the talk of others. In practice, however, it is common for some individuals to attempt to exert more control than others do, and for some individuals to be allowed or given more control than others, so that parties to an interaction are differentiated in the extent to which they control the talk.

In bureaucratized settings where many people become involved in sustaining a single focused interaction—e.g., courtrooms, classrooms, business meetings—talk usually is regulated by a system that explicitly allocated various types of control over turns at talk according to the social identities or roles of the participants. In the classroom the allocation of means for controlling turns at talk is asymmetrical, so that the person to whom the social identity of teacher is given has the right to make use of all forms of control, while those to whom the social identity of student has been assigned have few or none.

More specifically, the teacher determines who will speak next, and because a student must respond when called on, or not at all, the teacher also determines when a student will speak. This determination of who will speak next is not accomplished so much through focused address as through naming the next speaker. But it is also accomplished by virtue of the teacher's position as the only validating addressed recipient of student talk. Whomever the teacher focuses attention on has the floor, and whenever the teacher withdraws that attention, the student no longer has the floor.

It is this same position as sole validating addressed recipient that provides the teacher with control over the ends of students' turns at talk. While it is understood that teachers can interrupt them with their own talk, which they do not allow students to do to one another or to them, it is still generally not appropriate for teachers to do so once they have given students the floor. But it is common for teachers to have their attention focused on a student who is speaking, and to then have their attention drawn to the actions of another student, which effectively cuts off the speech of the first student.

In these ways then, the means for controlling turns at talk available in Anglo interaction are associated with the social identity of teacher in the classroom. Thus the differentiation of speakers in the extent of their use of such means, which normally emerges in the course of conversation and usually involves an association between higher status and greater control, is crystallized and institutionalized in the classroom.

The Warm Springs community patterns of interactional organization suggest that Warm Springs Indians are not accustomed to having to appeal to a single individual for permission to speak but rather to determining for themselves whether they will speak. Nor are they accustomed to having only one individual (the teacher) as their sole addressed recipient, but rather to more general address. And in the classroom, the teacher who has this control is not a familiar member of the community, but an outsider whose behavior is strange and unpredictable in many respects.

The Indian children are also not accustomed to a system for regulating turns at talk that always requires them to respond immediately if they are to respond at all. The teacher does not function within a framework that allows for the longer pauses between speakers' turns at talk that the Indian children observe in large-scale community events. The teacher is likely to allow too little time for a response before calling on another student or asking another question. The possibility that a child might respond to the question somewhat later in the sequential development of a class discussion is not likely to occur to the teacher. Such a response would in all likelihood not even be recognized as meaningful.

The system for regulating talk that is maintained in the classroom is also not compatible with many of the socialization practices within the Warm Springs community that were discussed in Chapter 5. The children are not oriented toward a single adult authority, being cared for by a number of adults and older children as they are. Partly because of this, Warm Springs children do not compete with one another for parental attention. They are expected to become more self-sufficient at younger ages, and to cooperate with older brothers and sisters and cousins in providing mutual companionship and care. For all of these reasons Warm Springs Indian children are less likely than Anglo children to be motivated to compete with one another for the teacher's attention.

And finally, the children are raised in an environment that discourages drawing attention to oneself by acting as though one is better than another. The efforts children are expected to make to get the teacher's attention to be given a turn at talk require them to draw attention to themselves, to lay claim to knowing more than their peers, and to demonstrate a desire to display that knowledge, all of which is unseemly by Indian adult standards for behavior.

For all of the above reasons, talking out of turn is also incompatible with Indian community norms, so it is not surprising that Indian students interrupt less often and do not attempt to speak when another student has been given a turn. Such actions are inconsistent with the tendency to allow individuals control over their own turns, and over their own behavior generally. The Indian children do not see others talking out of turn in the Warm Springs community. Furthermore, such violations also draw attention to the violator, just as other efforts to get the floor do, and as I have indicated, most Warm Springs Indians do not feel comfortable drawing attention to themselves.

Finally, the relatively more equal distribution of turns at talk among Indian students is also in keeping with behavior in the Indian community. This is what the children see in adult interactions. Talking too frequently or for too long is again likely to be seen as drawing attention to oneself and acting as though one is better than others, particularly in a young person. Raising one's hand quickly and often to indicate one knows the answer, which in turn leads to talking more, is associated with academic excellence among Anglos. But among Indian students such behavior is also interpreted as putting oneself above others.

Participant Structures

Thus far I have argued that Indian students withdraw from classroom interaction because it requires them to behave in ways that are incompatible with Warm Springs community members' notions of socially appropriate behavior. And I have tried to show how Indian behavior in the classroom is consistent with both Warm Springs adult behavior in face-to-face interaction, and the ways in which Warm Springs children are socialized in the community.

Most of the discussion of students as speakers that has been presented so far is drawn from encounters where the teacher is engaged in interaction with the whole class or a small group. But as is explained in Chapter 6, these are only two of several ways of organizing interaction that have been referred to as participant structures.

When a comparison of Indian and Anglo behavior is made across the various participant structures used for organizing interaction, it is possible to see that the Indian students participate more actively in some than in others. They pay more attention and talk more in those participant structures that minimize the features identified as typical of Anglo interaction and that maximize the possibility of regulating talk in a manner more characteristic of Warm Springs Indian interaction.

Indian students participate much less than Anglo students when the whole class is engaged in interaction with the teacher. Indian first graders are most reluctant to speak when they must assume the teacher's position to do so by standing up in front of and facing their peers, and, in some cases, fielding questions from them. The main opportunity for assuming the central position at the first-grade level occurs in the activity of Show and Tell. Most Anglo children at this age are at least a little shy about getting up before the class. But the Indian first graders are so reluctant to volunteer for Show and Tell that one teacher reported having dropped it altogether after several years of no success with it.

At the sixth-grade level, the Show and Tell format is used for individual reports as well as for activities resembling Show and Tell in which, for example, students might bring interesting newspaper articles to tell the class about. While this format was used frequently in the Anglo sixth-grade classroom, it was not used at all in the Indian sixth-grade classroom, again because the teacher had so little success with it.

The small group participant structure, in which the teacher engaged in interaction with a small number of students, also meets with little enthusiasm among the Indian students. Here, too, the Indian students participate much less than the non-Indian students. As indicated in Chapter 6, it is in the use of this participant structure that one most often sees students being called on one after another, regardless of whether they have raised their hands to indicate they wish to respond. When turn taking is handled in this way, Indian students much more often than Anglo students simply do not respond at all.

In the variant of the small group participant structure at the sixth-grade level, namely the group project, Indian students respond very differently. Here they are given the opportunity to control their own interaction. The group project is not normally used at the first-grade level, presumably because it is assumed that the children are not yet capable of sustaining a focused encounter by themselves, particularly one involving the coordination of six or seven students' actions in carrying out a task. But at my request, the first-grade teachers in whose classes I observed did arrange such encounters on a one-time basis, so I had the opportunity to compare the six-year olds engaged in group projects. At the sixth-grade level the group project is used for a variety of activities ranging from creating murals, to production of a class newspaper, to the construction of battery-run motors.

The Indian student verbal participation in group projects was not only much greater than in either whole-class or small-groups encounters, but also qualitatively different. As a rule, one could not determine who had been appointed as leaders of the Indian groups on the basis of the organization of interaction, and when the students were asked to pick a leader, they usually ignored that instruction and got on with the task at hand. In essence, they transformed the group-project organizational format so that it could no longer even be said to be a variant of the small-group participant structure. There was never any conflict over who should be directing activity or over who should be carrying out what task. Suggestions were either ignored or supported verbally and carried out. The students worked quickly and effectively, and completed their tasks without intervention from the teacher. They often turned the activity into a competition between the groups, verbalizing their desire to finish what they were doing ahead of other groups.

The Anglo students' behavior in group-project activities was quite different. Their leaders were readily identifiable by their manner of attempting to control the turns at talk and the actions of the others. When asked to select leaders they took the assignment to heart, but had difficulty in agreeing on how to accomplish this. They often disagreed about how to carry out their tasks and the leaders often had difficulty maintaining their authority. The Anglo students occasionally found it necessary to ask the teacher to intervene in their disputes, if the teacher had not already done so. Invariably, for any given task, some groups would not have completed the task in the time allotted by the teacher. The Anglo students took interest in the activities of groups other than their own, and were obviously observing them to compare their work with their own, but there was not the sort of open and explicit competition between groups that was initiated by the Indian students.

Perhaps the most striking differences between the Anglo and In-

dian students in their involvement in and use of the various participant structures was in relation to the one-to-one encounters between
the teacher and individual students through which students were
given help with their schoolwork. These encounters typically occurred while the students were working at their desks on reading or
writing assignments. Students usually initiated such encounters by
approaching the teacher at the teacher's desk, or raising their hands
to signal to the teacher that they wished the teacher to approach.
The Indian students at both the first- and sixth-grade levels made
much more use of this optional encounter than did the Anglo students. It was almost as if they were attempting to compensate for
their lack of communication with the teacher when the whole class
or small groups met with her. In sum, then, the Warm Springs Indian children participated much more actively in one-to-one encounters and in group projects than in lessons where the teacher met
with the whole class or in small groups.

In encounters between the teacher and the whole class or a small
group, those features which have been identified as distinctive to
Anglo organization of interaction are most in evidence. It is in these
participant structures that the teacher exercises greatest control over
who will talk, when they will talk, and what they will talk about. In
these arrangements the children have the least control over their
own turns at talk. In the Show and Tell variant of the whole-class
participant structure the children themselves are being asked to
learn to assume the controlling position that the teacher normally
occupies. These participant structures, then, are the least compatible
with Warm Springs' ways of organizing interaction, and it is accordingly understandable that the Indian children participate in them
as little as they do.

In the group-project variant of the small-group participant structure, by contrast, the Indian students have an opportunity to regulate their own turns at talk as they wish. In this context they make
little use of leaders, so that students are able to control their turns at
talk, and avoid attempting to control the talk of others. The Indian
children's high degree of involvement in group projects is due, then,
to the opportunity there to regulate interaction in a manner to which
they are accustomed in the Warm Springs community.

The one-to-one encounters between teacher and student similarly allow students greater control over their contribution to the interaction. Students are able to determine to some degree the point at
which such encounters will take place, and the specific topical concern that will be taken up. In these involvements the child is the
only other possible speaker besides the teacher and does not have to

compete with other students to get the teacher's attention. And children in one-to-one encounters with the teacher need not be concerned with avoiding drawing attention to themselves by talking more than others. In sum, it is evident that the Indian children participate most actively in those participant structures which allow them to approximate the modes of interaction that are most familiar to them from their experiences in the Warm Springs community.

One can see these same preferences expressed in the children's playground activities during recess periods, and before and after school.

At the first-grade level one of the two recess periods is regularly devoted to physical activities supervised by the teacher, ranging from exercises on the jungle gym to organized games. In contrast to the Anglo children, the Warm Springs Indian children demonstrate a strong preference for team games and races, engaging in them with enthusiasm. But they show reluctance to function as leaders in games that require one person to control the activities of others, as in Farmer in the Dell and Follow the Leader. It is interesting to note that games requiring such control provide children with practice in singly exerting authority over others, just as Show and Tell and group projects with leaders do in the classroom. Anglo children engage in these games with enthusiasm, and during free periods are sometimes seen playing school, where one child assumes the role of teacher, a game the Indian children do not play.

During free recess periods, Indian children play more team games than Anglo children. There is more mingling of children of different ages and grades on the Indian playground as well. This is largely due to the fact that most of the children have siblings and cousins in the other grades who are accustomed to playing together at one another's homes. The Indian children are also able to sustain interactions involving more children for longer periods of time than the Anglo children of this age. This may be due in part to their greater degree of involvement with older children.

At the sixth-grade level there are regular physical education periods instead of physical activities controlled by the classroom teachers. The sixth-grade Indian students' behavior during recess periods differs from that of the Anglo students in a manner similar to that of the first graders. By the time they reach this age, the Indian students regularly engage in team sports and spend more of their time in such activities than the Anglo students. In keeping with the seasonal cycle of the most popular team sports, the males play football constantly in the fall months, and both males and females play basketball and baseball in the months that follow. Once again, the Indian students are capable of sustaining such team activities with more children involved for longer periods of time.

This preference for team acitivity and success in sustaining interaction without adult supervision is expressed largely through physical activity monitored in the visual channel when it occurs on the playground. But analogous behavior is expressed in both the visual and the auditory channels in classroom infrastructure activity.

The greater involvement of Indian students in the interaction between peers that flourishes covertly around the activities of the official structure organized by the teacher has already been discussed in the section on paying attention. What is relevant here is that in Indian classrooms the lines of infrastructure communication are more equally distributed. All of the Indian children were involved in talking to one another, whereas in the Anglo classrooms there were always one or two students who were clearly peripheral to peer interaction and rarely talked to anyone.

In addition, in the Anglo classrooms, particularly at the sixth-grade level, most of the communication of most children was with two or three other students who were usually seated close by. And during recess periods these students were usually seen with one or two of those they usually talked to in the classroom. By contrast, the Indian students each engaged in communication with a greater number of students, and did not limit themselves to those seated close by. The Indian students' greater range was very much facilitated by their greater use of nonverbal communication in the visual channel discussed earlier.

Nor could the more equal distribution of connections in the Indian students' interactional network be attributed to the teacher's seating plan, for in both Indian and Anglo sixth-grade classrooms the teachers allowed the students preferential seating, so they were able to sit next to those they chose.

There is one qualification to this general pattern, however, that should be noted. At both the first- and sixth-grade levels, Indian students' infrastructure encounters were more sexually segregated, in that they less often communicated with members of the opposite sex. While such segregation is usual among Anglo children also, it was still manifest in a more extreme form in the Indian peer interactions. On the playground, in the cafeteria, and even in choosing seats in the music room, greater sexual segregation was observed among Indian students. Such segregation is also the norm in large-scale public events within the community, where husbands and wives who come together more often than not separate upon arrival to join kinsmen of the same sex. And it is manifest in ritual as well, where roles are sex-specific and spatially separated.

Thus the more equal distribution of peer exchanges among the Indian students is primarily in reference to the same sex. Yet even in regard to attention directed to the opposite sex, the Indian children were more likely to have contact with a greater number of classroom members.

And finally as was the case in group projects and playround activities, the Indian students were able to sustain infrastructure interactions involving more students for a longer time without the interaction breaking down because of conflict or too many people attempting to control the talk.

Earlier in this discussion on the behavior of students as speakers, it was argued that the use of devices for controlling the turns at talk of others are incompatible with the Warm Springs Indian preference for minimization of control over the turns at talk of others. Because such control over others' talk is allocated to the teacher in the classroom to varying degrees, Indian students withdraw from participant structures in which the exercise of such control is most in evidence, preferring neither to be controlled by the teacher nor to be put in the leadership position of controlling others. On the playground at recesses, one finds a similar preference among Indian children for activities that do not involve one person controlling the activities of others.

Related to these preferences is the greater competence the Indian students demonstrate in maintaining interaction among a greater number of children for longer periods of time without the supervision of a leader. This ability is apparent not only in the group-project activities set up by the teacher as part of official classroom interaction, but also in the children's play at recess and in the infrastructure encounters in the classroom.

The Indian children's tendency to distribute their infrastructure involvements among a greater number of children than Anglo children also facilitates their ability to maintain interactions in this way, as does their experience in play with older kinsmen at home, where the children as a group are held collectively responsible for their actions. All in all, they have a great deal of practice in interaction that does not involve control by a single individual, so that their experience in any one of the situations described increases their ability to maintain interaction in the other situations.

The Anglo children, by contrast have more difficulty regulating interaction among more than three or four children in all of the contexts discussed. However, they learn to use leaders to regulate interaction in games with leaders, and in the classroom interactions. This in turn prepares them for the hierarchically organized interactions of the occupational worlds they will enter. Thus while there is continuity and consistency among the various spheres of activity through which the Anglo children are socialized, and between their socializing experiences and the adult world of work they will enter, for the Warm Springs Indian children this is not the case. The Indian children instead experience conflict between their community socializing experiences and classroom socialization—a conflict that continues into adult life.

8

Conclusion

Recapitulation

Certain characteristics of both attention structuring and speaker changes associated with talk as a mode of communication are probably universal and based in the shared biological heritage of the human species. Other such characteristics are culturally variable and result from learning processes through which socially appropriate communicative behavior is acquired.

Warm Springs Indian children learn socially appropriate ways of conveying attention and regulating turns at talk in their homes and their community before they come to school. They imitate the communicative behavior of Warm Springs adults that was described in Chapter 4. And they are deliberately socialized so that they acquire skills in the use of the visual and auditory channels of communication in culturally distinctive ways. Thus in regard to both the structuring of attention and the allocation of turns at talk, Warm Springs Indian children learn culturally distinctive systems for socially appropriate communication.

At the age of six, the Indian children enter a classroom where the organization of interaction is Anglo in its hierarchical structure, and in the control of talk that one individual exercises. The relative use of the visual and auditory channels and the organization of participant structures for the presentation of curriculum have been developed for the Anglo middle-class child. The organization of class-room interaction at the first-grade level is designed to fit with or build on the interactional skills the Anglo children have acquired during their first six years of life. That organization does not, however, completely fit or build on the interactional skills acquired by the Warm Springs Indian children.

Anglo and Indian children are similar in many ways due to a shared developmental sequence deriving from their common biological heritage as humans. They also share the influence of Western, or American, culture. But they differ as well, due to cultural differences in early childhood socialization that are not taken into account in the development of school curriculum.

There is evidence of Indian students' lack of comprehension in the structure of discourse between the teacher and those students. Perhaps it would be more accurate to say that one can see how the teacher defines the Indian children as noncomprehending, by her failure to ratify their efforts to get the floor. It seems most likely that the Indian students are experiencing communicative interference on a number of different levels.

In the structuring of attention, and in the regulation of talk, there are differences between Anglo and Warm Springs Indians that result in miscommunication between student and teacher in the Indian classrooms. Those differences contribute to the general uncertainty Indian children experience as they find they do not understand the teacher, and the teacher does not understand them.

While I have focused on cultural differences in attention structuring and the regulation of talk, it is clear that there are cultural differences in other aspects of the communicative process that also contribute to the teachers' definition of the Indian child's speech as inappropriate. First, there are dialect differences that were not within the scope of the research discussed in the preceding chapters that may cause the teacher to misunderstand the child, or to define what she hears as unacceptable.

Second, there are differences in rules for appropriate discourse, or for the ways a speaker builds on or relates to the utterances of prior speakers. Cultural differences in discourse rules were also not a focus of this research, yet there is evidence of such differences in the greater use of general rather than focused address among Indian adults, and in the post-ponement of responses to questions.

Finally, there are differences in cultural knowledge that can contribute to the breakdown of communication wherever one speaker has no direct knowledge of what another is speaking about. Because Anglo and Indian spheres of interaction are largely segregated from one another, Indian students and Anglo teachers have little direct experience with one another's activities. Thus their shared knowledge is less than that between Anglo teachers and Anglo students.

In all of these ways, then, Indian children experience a culturally alien environment when they enter the school. It is little wonder that they withdraw from classroom interaction as they do.

In considering the relevance of the findings in this particular school system and Indian cultural context for other groups of Indians and other ethnic or minority communities, such as those of blacks and Chicanos, I would suggest that students from such backgrounds will be defined as similarly inadequate in their efforts to pay attention and to get the floor in classroom interaction. The specific sources of this inadequacy will vary in keeping with the cultural diversity among the various groups involved.

Other ethnic minority students are likely to resemble the Indian students of Warm Springs in an overall disinclination to participate in official classroom interaction with a concomitant greater interest in and involvement with their peers in infrastructure interactions. And they are likely to be defined by the teacher more often than Anglo middle-class students as inappropriate in their efforts to sustain both the addressor and addressee ends of the floor, with that inadequacy being conveyed by two things: (1) These students' speaking will less often be integrated into the sequential structure of talk. The comprehensibility of the teachers' speakings will require or indicate the teachers' having heard students' speakings less often in proportion to the amount of speaking the students actually do. And teachers will more often repeat what they have said, again indicating the nonacceptability of student responses. (2) The students will more often be explicitly informed that they are behaving inappropriately as listeners and speakers. They will be chastised for not paying attention, for talking out of turn, or for failing to talk when they are supposed to.

A study suggesting that minority students other than Indians have similar experiences in relation to floor holding is the recent report of the U.S. Commission on Civil Rights on "Differences in Teacher Interaction with Mexican American and Anglo Students" (U.S. Commission on Civil Rights, 1973). While the categories used in discussing differences in teacher interaction are difficult to compare with distinctions made in this study, one finding in particular is nevertheless suggestive. In a survey based on observation in 429 classrooms in which the proportion of Mexican-American students varied, the investigators found: "The average Anglo student spends about 27 percent more time speaking in the classroom than the average Chicano student" (U.S. Commission, 1972:40). To illustrate what they took to be the source of this disparity, the Commission staff noted:

> One Chicano sat toward the back in a corner and volunteered several answers. At one point the teacher did not even acknowledge, much less reinforce, his answer. At another time he volunteered an answer which was perfectly suitable. Yet the teacher stated: "Well, yes uh huh, but can anyone else put it in different terms?" The teacher then called on an Anglo boy who gave the same basic response with very little paraphrasing. The teacher then beamed and exclaimed: "Yes, that's it exactly." (U.S. Commission, 1973:40–41)

The orientation of the Commission Report is such that cultural differences of the sort considered in this study are not dealt with in attempting to account for the disparities discussed. The impression is given that the disparities are due to what is typically referred to as "discrimination." But as I have tried to show, even where teachers are well intentioned, the results are similar, because the minority students' efforts to communicate are often incomprehensible to the teacher and cannot be assimilated into the framework within which the teacher operates. The teacher, then, must be seen as uncomprehending, just as the students are. And it is primarily by virtue of the teacher's position and authority that the students and not the teacher come to be defined as the ones who do not understand.

While students from other than an Anglo, middle-class cultural background are likely to be similarly defined as inadequate interactants in the way suggested above, the sources or causes of their being defined in this way are likely to differ in keeping with differences in their cultural background. Thus while Warm Springs Indian students speak too softly, hesitate too long before speaking, and engage in too much visually received signaling from the point of view of teacher expectations, Indians of other reservations and students from various black and Chicano groups may be similarly defined as inadequate on other grounds.

For example, black students in classrooms in San Diego, California reportedly engage in a great deal of loud talking when interacting with one another. Their talk is louder than that of Anglo students and is seen as interfering more with other classroom interactions. But because they are accustomed to this in their own community situations, they are more practiced in separating "message" from "noise" at higher levels of noise than Anglo students are, and do not experience the loud talking as distracting. Nevertheless they are disciplined sharply by Anglo teachers for engaging in it, because of the teacher's working assumption that the sound level it entails is disruptive.

Practical Implications

This study has implications for changes in the education of ethnic minority children regarding who does the teaching, what is taught, and how the teaching is carried out.

Teachers

For many years there has been a call for minority teachers in minority classrooms from a number of sources. It has been suggested, for example, that Indian teachers will be less likely to misinterpret Indian children, because of the cultural background shared by teacher and student. And Indian children are thought to be more likely to identify with, pay attention to, and establish rapport with teachers that are more like themselves.

Some have argued that the fact that a teacher is Indian will not automatically guarantee a better relationship with Indian students than an Anglo teacher would have. Often the Indians who become teachers have become so assimilated to the Anglo world in order to get their education that they too are culturally quite different from the children they teach. And some of these teachers are thought to be too hard on the children because they assume that if they themselves could "make it" without any coddling, then the students they teach can also.

The existence of such teachers does not mean that all Indian teachers are this way, however, or that teachers being trained now will be that way. And in practice, the many Indian aides hired through federal funding to reservation school districts have been neither assimilated to mainstream Anglo middle-class culture, nor harsh with Indian children.

The federal funding of teachers' aides suggests a public policy supportive of Indian teachers in the classroom. But too few of these aides are becoming the actual teachers in control of the classroom. There are other programs designed to sensitize Anglo teachers to the culturally distinctive backgrounds of the children they teach or will teach. The results of this study suggest that there are some crucial aspects of culturally distinctive communicative behavior that cannot be readily internalized by Anglo teachers. Thus the findings presented here argue in favor of giving priority to the facilitation of movement of Indian adults into teaching positions in Indian classrooms.

It is likely that the culturally appropriate listening behavior of Warm Springs Indian children, and other minority children like them, would be particularly difficult for the Indian children to change, and for Anglo teachers to themselves interpret or produce. To be more explicit, I am claiming that Anglo teachers will have difficulty feeling that they are being attended to if they are not looked at often, that they will have difficulty allowing longer pauses after they pose questions, and so on—even if they are aware that the Indian students are functioning differently as listeners.

There are several reasons why the cultural differences in listening behavior are probably particularly resistant to being coped with by Anglo teachers. Nonverbal behavior in humans is generally less subject to our conscious monitoring than language. It is more under the control of the older brain, the limbic cortex (Chevalier-Skolnikoff, 1974). Language is more under the control of the outer cerebral cortex that is evolutionarily more recent, and more generally associated with conscious thought processes that the limbic cortex.

The nonverbal behavior involved in management of the body in social interaction is more fully learned at an earlier age than language, which may in turn be related to the earlier maturation of the parts of the brain that process nonverbal behavior. Nonverbal behavior also seems to be culturally conservative in nature, or generally less subject to cultural change than other domains of behavior. Thus North American Indian demeanor is generally similar among many tribes: the degree of facial expressiveness, the form and positioning of hand gestures, patterns of gaze, and manner of holding the body and walking are shared to a large degree among various Indian groups, while they have differed greatly in language, dress, mode of adaptation to the environment and other areas of learned activity.

Nonverbal patterns of behavior are clearly acquired through the socialization process, as evidenced by the changes in gestural patterns between one generation and another among immigrants in this country (Efron, 1941). But they are very slow to change among people who are socially segregated and do not have regular contact or identify with people who display nonverbal patterns that are different from their own.

Thus it is likely that Indian children will continue to convey attention in culturally distinctive ways for some time to come, and will continue to benefit from the presence of Indian teachers in the classroom who themselves listen in a similar manner and interpret their behavior as it would be interpreted in their homes.

Curriculum Content

For some time culturally relevant curriculum materials have been recommended for children from ethnic minority backgrounds, and some of these materials have been very successful in reservation learning environments. The results of this study reinforce the arguments for the need for such materials in Indian classrooms. There were many instances of nonresponsiveness on the part of Indian children that seemed related to the total irrelevance of the curriculum content to their lives. The materials in the classroom presuppose a cultural background that is different from the background actually acquired by the Indian children.

It is possible to object to the use of culturally relevant curriculum material on the grounds that children from ethnic minority backgrounds will then be learning something different from what their Anglo counterparts learn, and will through this be placed at a disadvantage on tests measuring academic achievement, and ultimately on the job market. Yet clearly the most basic skills taught in the schools, like reading, writing and mathematics, do not depend on Anglo middle-class content. Why shouldn't reservation students learn about the history and political structure of their reservation, rather than the history of the state which less directly affects their daily lives? Clearly too the broad rather than compartmentalized introduction of culturally relevant curriculum materials would be much more effective if it were taught by Indian teachers, who were themselves in a position to clarify and elaborate on such materials. Thus who teaches and what is taught are closely related. Yet the question remains: who will develop these curriculum materials? Much of the burden for such development has fallen on the classroom teacher who typically is overburdened and overworked with daily teaching responsibilities. This question will be addressed in the last section of this chapter.

Teaching Methods

It should be apparent from the preceding chapters that the implications of this study are greater for the area teaching methodology than the other two aspects of the classroom learning process that have already been discussed. Surprisingly little attention has been given to the teaching methods used in teaching ethnic minority students in this country, particularly when the notion of culturally relevant curriculum materials has been around as long as it has. It is as if we have been able to recognize that there are cultural differences in what people learn, but not in how they learn.

In this book I have dealt with one dimension of teaching method, namely the behavioral and social organization of face-to-face interaction. In Chapter 1, I discussed the idea that the transmission of culture is accomplished through communication in face-to-face interaction. There is invariably a structure to that interaction which is used by humans to provide a framework for the transmission of culture. That structure organizes verbal and nonverbal behavior.

While some characteristics of the organization of interaction are probably universal, there is also cultural variability in some of its aspects. Children learn through both the process of interaction and the organization of interaction. Indian and Anglo children have already learned different systems for the organization of interaction by the time they come to school. In the Warm Springs grade school the Indian children show a preference for structures that are more like the structures they have learned or acquired in their preschool community experience.

The most obvious practical implication of these findings is that in Indian classrooms the participant structures preferred by the Indian students can be used successfully to a greater extent for the transmission of curriculum content than they now are. Thus the group-project format, in which the children have more control over their own interaction, may be used for a greater diversity of purposes and at younger ages in Indian classrooms. And Indian children may particularly benefit from greater opportunity to engage in one-to-one contact with teachers and aides. Indian students can also be allowed to help one another more in their academic work.

Some Indian parents may feel that such adaptation to Indian ways of organizing interaction may only make it more difficult for the Indian children when they must eventually interact through Anglo ways of organizing interaction. Where this is a real concern, ways may be found to ease the Indian children more gradually and less crucially into patterns of interaction with which they are not comfortable. Thus for example, the children whose natural leadership ability is apparent may be encouraged to lead activities with their peers in such a way that they must get up before the others and speak regarding a concern of interest to all the students, as a class president might in conducting the planning of a class picnic. Other children may feel more at ease following the lead of someone they trust and look up to. And where individual effort contributes to a group goal, as in debate-like competitions, the Indian children may feel more comfortable putting themselves forward than they do when self-aggrandizement can be the only outcome of their efforts.

I do not mean to convey that the above suggestions will work in any Indian classroom, since there are many processes that affect the ultimate success or failure of efforts to teach. Rather, I am trying to suggest a process of thinking that can be useful in altering classroom learning environments so that they are more compatible with the cultural backgrounds of ethnic minority children who find those learning environments so unpalatable. The idea is to use knowledge of cultural developmental differences creatively in teaching.

Agents of Change

The question arises again that was raised in the last section: Who will undertake to carry out such innovations in the teaching metho-dology used in classrooms inhabited by ethnic minority children? Because the teacher is so immediately involved with her students, there is a tendency to direct arguments for attention to cultural variation in the socialization process toward the teacher, and to assume that the teacher can be creative and innovative with curricu-lum content and teaching methodology in the classroom. But teachers are usually expected to experiment with changes in their teaching in addition to the normal teaching duties that are already a strain on the mental and physical resources of the normal person.

If local school administrations support a minority community's demands for cultural sensitivity in the classroom, then the teachers have a right to expect a lot of support from those administrations in altering curriculum and teaching methods to make their learning en-vironments more responsive to the child from an ethnic minority background. Support does not just mean a pat on the back, but money and free time to develop materials.

Yet even if individual teachers are capable of developing new materials and new approaches, that is still not what they were trained primarily to do, and their individual efforts will not be insti-tutionalized without the involvement of other agents of change. It is important that federal funding of curriculum development for minority children continue, and that state boards of education facili-tate the dissemination of such materials through changes in the sta-tutes laying out statewide curriculum requirements. The universities that train the teachers who work in minority communities need to provide them with more specialized preparation for adapting their traditional teaching methods to culturally different communities. Above all, it is important that all of these agents of change be structurally linked with and responsive to the minority communities' goals for their children, and their knowledge of what their children need in order to grow and learn.

References

Barth, F., 1969, Introduction. *Ethnic Groups and Boundaries*. Boston: Little, Brown and Company, 9–38.

Berry, B. 1968 *The Education of American Indians*. Washington, D.C.: Office of Education, Bureau of Research.

Birdwhistell, R., 1970, *Kinesics and Context: Essays on Body Motion Communication*. Philadelphia: University of Pennsylvania Press.

Blount, B., 1972, Aspects of Luo socialization. *Language in Society*, 1, 235–248.

Braroe, N., 1970, *Change and Identity: Patterns of Interaction in an Indian-White Community*. Ph.D. dissertation, Department of Anthropology, University of Illinois.

Chance, M. R. A., 1962, An interpretation of some agonistic postures: the role of "cut off" acts and postures. *Symp. Zool. Soc. London*, 8:71–89.

——— and R. R. Larsen (eds.), 1975, *The Structure of Social Attention*. London: Wiley.

Chevalier-Skolnikoff, S., 1974, Facial expression of emotion in nonhuman primates. In P. Ekman (ed.), *Darwin and Facial Expression: A Century of Research in Review*. New York: Academic Press, pp. 11–90.

Chomsky, N., 1959, A review of B. F. Skinner's *Verbal Behavior*. *Language*, 35:26–58.

Coan, C. F., 1922, The adoption of the reservation policy in the Pacific Northwest, 1835–1855. *Quarterly of the Oregon Historical Society*, 23:1–38.

Condon, W. and W. Ogston, 1971, Speech and body motion synchrony of the speaker-hearer. In D. L. Horton and J. J. Jenkins (eds.), *The Perception of Language*. Columbus: Charles E. Merrill, 224–56.

Cook, S. F., 1955, The epidemic of 1830–1833 in California and Oregon. *University of California Publications in American Archaeology and Ethnology,* 53:303–25.

DuBois, C., 1938, *The Feather Cult of the Middle Columbia.* General Series in Anthropology, No. 7, Menasha, Wisconsin.

Duncan, S., 1972, Some signals and rules for taking speaking turns in conversation. *J. Pers. Soc. Psychol.,* 23, 283–92.

Efron, D., 1941, *Gesture and Environment.* New York: King's Crown Press.

Ekman, P., 1974, Cross-cultural studies of facial expression. In P. Ekman (ed.), *Darwin and Facial Expression: A Century of Research in Review.* New York: Academic Press, pp. 169–222.

French, D., 1961, Wasco-Wishram. In E. Spicer (ed.), *Perspectives in American Indian Culture Change.* Chicago: University of Chicago Press, 337–430.

French, K., 1955, *Culture Segments and Variation in Contemporary Social Ceremonialism on the Warm Springs Reservation, Oregon.* Ph.D. Dissertation, Columbia University.

Goffman, E., 1963, *Behavior in Public Places.* New York: Macmillan Co.

Goodenough, W., 1976, Multi-culturalism as the normal human experience. In M. Gibson (ed.), Anthropological Perspectives on Multi-cultural Education, *Anthropology and Education Quarterly,* Vol. VII, No. 4, 4–7.

Gumperz, J., 1977, The conversational analysis of interethnic communication. In E. Ross (ed.), *Interethnic Encounters.* Proceedings of the Southern Anthropological Society, University of Georgia Press.

Hall, E., 1966, *The Hidden Dimension.* New York: Doubleday.

Hymes, D., 1966, Two types of linguistic relativity. In W. Bright (ed.), *Sociolinguistics.* The Hague: Mouton, 114–165.

——, 1967, On communicative competence MS.

——, 1968, The wife who goes out like a man: Reinterpretation of a Clackamas Chinook Myth. *Studies in Semiotics,* 7(3):173–99.

Jacobs, M., 1929, Northwest Sahaptin texts. *University of Washington Publications in Anthropology,* 2:175–244.

——, 1958, *Clackamas Chinook Texts, Part I.* Bloomington, Indiana University Research Center in Anthropology, Folklore, and Linguistics, No. 8.

Kendon, A., 1967, Some functions of gaze direction in social interaction. *Acta Psychologica,* 26, 1–47.

La Barre, W., 1947, The cultural basis of emotion and gestures. *Journal of Personality,* 16.1 (September), 49–68.

McDermott, R. P., 1974, Achieving school failure. In G. Spindler (ed.), *Education and Cultural Process.* New York: Holt, Rinehart and Winston, 82–118.

Mehan, H. 1979, Learning Lessons: Social Organization in the Classroom. Cambridge: Harvard University Press.

Montagu, A., 1971, Touching: The Human Significance of the Skin. New York: Harper and Row.

Murdock, G., 1962, Tenino shamanism. *Ethnology,* 165–171.

Pitcairn, T. and I. Eibl-Eibesfeldt, 1976, Concerning the evolution of nonverbal communication in man. In M. Hahn and E. Simmel (eds.), *Communicative Behavior and Evolution*, 81–114.

Philips, S., 1974a *The Invisible Culture: Communication in Classroom and Community on the Warm Springs Indian Reservation*. Ph.D. Dissertation. University of Pennsylvania.

Philips, S., 1974b, Literacy as a mode of communication on the Warm Springs Indian Reservation. In E. H. Lenneberg and E. Lenneberg (eds.), *Foundations of Language Development*, Vol. 2, 367,382. New York: Academic Press.

———, 1975a, Teasing, punning, and putting people on. *Working Papers in Sociolinguistics*, No. 28. Austin: Southwest Educational Development Laboratory.

———, 1975b, Warm Springs Indian time: How the regulation of participation affects the progression of events. In R. Bauman and J. Sherzer (eds.), *Explorations in the Ethnography of Speaking*. Cambridge: Cambridge University Press, 92–109.

———, 1980, Sex Differences and Language. In B. Siegal (ed.), *Annual Review of Anthropology*, Vol. 9. Palo Alto: Annual Reviews, Inc., pp. 523–44.

———, 1981, Indian children in Anglo classrooms. In N. Wolfson and J. Manes (eds.), *The Language of Inequality*. Forthcoming.

Sacks, H., 1966–67, Lecture Notes.

Saks, H., E. Schegloff, and Gail Jefferson, 1974. A simplest systematics for the organization of turntaking for conversation. *Language* 50: 696–735.

Schegloff, E., 1972, Sequencing in conversational openings. In J. Gumperz and D. Hymes (eds.), *Directions in Sociolinguistics*. New York: Holt, Rinehart and Winston, 346–380.

Shafton, A., 1976, *Conditions of Awareness*. Portland, Oregon: Riverstone Press.

Spier, L., and E. Sapir, 1930, Wishram ethnography. *University of Washington Publications in Anthropology*, 3:151–300.

Stern, T. and J. Boggs, 1971, White and Indian Farmers on the Umatilla Indian Reservation. Special issue of *Northwest Anthropological Notes*: An Exploration of the reservation system in America, 5, 1:37–76.

U.S. Commission on Civil Rights, 1973, *Differences in Teacher Interaction with Mexican American and Anglo Students*.

White, L., 1949, The symbol: The origin and basis of human behavior. In *The Science of Culture*. Farrar, Strauss and Cudahy, Inc., pp. 22–39.

Yngve, V., 1970, On getting a word in edgewise. Paper read at Sixth Regional Meeting of the Chicago Linguistic Society, April, 1970.

Zentner, H., 1960, *Volume II.: Education*. Oregon State College Warm Springs Research Project.

Transcription Notational Devices

The transcription format used in excerpts from tape recordings in classrooms imitates the system developed by Gail Jefferson (Sacks Schegloff Jefferson, 1974):

[6(1) WS1–997]   Material in brackets or parentheses at the end of an excerpt identify the location of the quote on a tape.

/Grow. Grow/Grow   Material between slashes in the speech of two adjacent speakers shows when they are talking at the same time.

(how he does it)   Material inside parentheses in word form indicates the transcriber was not sure that this is what the speaker said.

( )	Empty parentheses indicate the transcriber heard speech, but could not decode it.
(2 sec.)	Parentheses with numbers of seconds enclosed indicate lengths of pauses that are two seconds or more in length.
——	A dash marks a pause that is noticeable, but of less than two seconds in length.
Student²	Within a given excerpt, the same student voice will always be assigned the same raised number.
. . . .	A sequence of dots indicates that talk within the turn being quoted has been excised.

Index

ISBN 0-88133-694-7

90000